Praise for *Climb:*

"A great anthology that captures the humor, epics, and magic of the game we play."
—Sir Chris Bonington, acclaimed British mountaineer and author

"Climbers usually have more on their minds than putting pen to paper, such as getting to the next route alive. This lack of time or concentration leads to many dull accounts for those who lazily rise to the occasion. But here, in *Climb,* the editors have gone to the trouble of scouring the vast body of climbing literature and pulling forth some of the most varied and lyrical pieces of our strange pastime. It's unusual and wonderful to see an account of an ancient French adventure coupled with an eloquent book review-and, of course, all sorts of other fascinating material. Well done!"
—Steve Roper, noted climber, author, and historian of the Sierra Nevada and founding editor of *Ascent*

"This collection of mountain tales brings together some of the finest and most important stories in climbing history. I am delighted to rediscover many of my favorite treasures, and surprised that I'd overlooked a few that were equally good. Here is mountaineering distilled to its essence."
—John Harlin, climber, author, and editor of *American Alpine Journal*

"Kerry and Cameron Burns have compiled an eclectic mix of articles and short stories that span the rich history of our sport, from playful humor to the distinctly serious. For me, one gem is a previously unpublished account of the first British ascent of the Bonatti Pillar, which provides new insight of both events and the (now legendary) players of this simply epic tale."
—Lindsay Griffin, acclaimed British mountaineer

"If you want to learn why the best climbing narratives transcend the adventure genre and speak through the ages, read *Climb*."
—John Long, legendary climber and adventure writer

"Glistening narratives from climbing's best story tellers."
—John Middendorf, American big wall climber and developer
    of climbing equipment

"The Burnses have done a magnificent job of distilling the climbing experience in their selection of writings for this anthology. These accounts by various authors from the 14th century to the present recount every kind of tale from early traditional alpine ascents (to reach summits) to the more varied forms of climbing we now see in the 21st century.

    This book is more than just a collection of stories about climbing. These epics recount triumph and tragedy as well as the foibles of humankind itself, exploring the depths of the human psyche. Add this one to your book collection!"
—Ed Cooper, American climbing author and mountain
    photographer

CLIMB

Tales of Man Versus Boulder, Crag, Wall, and Peak

Edited by
Kerry L. Burns and Cameron M. Burns

FALCONGUIDES

GUILFORD, CONNECTICUT
HELENA, MONTANA

AN IMPRINT OF GLOBE PEQUOT PRESS

All photos by Cameron M. Burns unless otherwise noted

Project editor: David Legere
Text design: Sheryl Kober
Layout artist: Maggie Peterson

Library of Congress Cataloging-in-Publication Data

Climb : tales of man versus boulder, crag, wall, and peak / edited by Kerry L. Burns and
Cameron M. Burns.
     p. cm.
  ISBN 978-0-7627-7149-3
  I. Mountaineering. 2. Rock climbing. I. Burns, Kerry L. II. Burns, Cameron.
  GV200.C584 2012
  796.522—dc23
                                                                  2011033824

Printed in the United States of America

10 9 8 7 6 5 4 3 2 1

To Mary Jessica Burns, née Murdoch,
for tolerating all this foolishness
with humor and unflagging support.

CONTENTS

ACKNOWLEDGMENTS

This book would not have been possible without help from many people.

First, a huge thank-you to Beth Heller, Adam McFarren, Alex Depta, and Gary Landeck at the American Alpine Club Library in Golden. Also, for inspiration and ideas, thanks go to David Stevenson, John Harlin III, Dougald MacDonald, Glen Denny, Steve Roper, Layton Kor, Allen Hill, John Catto, Stewart Green, Eric Bjornstad, and Ed and Debby Cooper. Thanks also to Jess Haberman at GPP for pushing us along through the gathering process.

We also want to thank Peter and Sue Burns, Jill Murdoch, Pat Webb, Heather and Rod Gough, Michael Burns and Jan Newall, and Rob and Kian Murdoch.

Thanks to our fellow adventurers: Ann, Zoe, and Mollie Burns; Mike, Penny, Jessie, Nattie, and Katie Sandy; Glenn, Gillian, Ryan, Kelsea, and Jamie Haste; Bob and Sylvia Robertson; Benny Bach; Angie Moquin; Charlie French; Amory Lovins; Luke and Mel Laeser; and Diana and Carlo Torres.

Thanks also to the handful of noted climbers/authors who endorsed this book, including: Ed Cooper, John Harlin III, Steve Roper, Chris Bonington, Lindsay Griffin, John Middendorf, John Long, and Pete Athans.

INTRODUCTION

The selection of stories you hold in your hands started out in an altogether different form—*Classic Climbing Stories*—that we pulled together for Lyons Press in 2005. While those stories were and remain fascinating, in late 2010 Globe Pequot Press suggested we take another look at the stories gathered therein. So we started looking around, primarily at more modern stories.

One of the remarkable things about climbing literature is its evolution, which has always reflected the evolution of the sport itself. Until about the early twentieth century, most climbing stories, for example, followed a fairly routine path: a description of the objective, the events of the ascent, then a bit of a summation—and maybe a brief mention of the wonder of nature and some Divine force.

By the early twentieth century, however, things had changed dramatically. Climbers (still mostly men) were not only talking about conquering features of the Earth's crust, they were also writing about everything from the mundane to the surreal to, wonderfully, the imagined (which has by far the biggest presence in climbing). We began to read about how fingers can hurt, how motivation can wane, and how uncertainty can play on psyches.

David Brower's 1939 retelling of his climb of the Yosemite Point Couloir with Morgan Harris and Torcom Bedayan is a great example. Certainly, there's a lot of the traditional climbing-story stuff going on, but Brower actually admits to "cheating" while climbing. Brower's account is no lynchpin in the art of climbing storytelling, but it points the way.

If you discount the 1940s because of World War II, what started in the 1930s continued in the 1950s and 1960s, and certainly in the 1970s and 1980s. Climbers weren't just writing about fear and uncertainty. They were writing about how companions can stink (in both ways), how bodily functions can become urgent, and what the person on the other end of the rope might be thinking and/or saying, to the point of quoting his lines for him. We also got to hear about death and all its long-lasting consequences for the living.

Two important changes to the storytelling repertoire in the late twentieth century were dark and/or sarcastic humor and the increasing presence of female climbers. Stories also reflected the division of climbing into its various sub-activities: bouldering, sport climbing, traditional rock climbing, big wall climbing (in its various phases), ice climbing, mixed climbing, alpinism, etc.

In this collection we have gathered stories representative of all the most significant eras and most important genres (the climbing-book review, as Royal Robbins's piece shows, is indeed a major genre in and of itself), and we've also included several stories from other parts of the world, because although climbing can be an activity insulated from the rest of society, within the climbing community knowledge and stories are shared on a global basis.

Hopefully you won't regard the selections within as an oddball collection without rhyme or reason—our goal was to show off the richness that exists in climbing literature across the ages and around the globe. Happy reading.

—*Kerry L. Burns* and *Cameron M. Burns*

MIND GAMES (1984)

David Pagel

We had spent years laboring on the small bluffs of eastern Minnesota under the incredulous eyes of Lake Superior vacationers and St. Croix River valley tourists. "Crazy" they called us, as we clung to ropes the size of their pinkies and disappeared over precipices that loomed all of fifty feet over the spongy ground below. We liked to think of it as training. Two months of our summer dragged once more through this routine until at last, Jim and I decided it was time to pack up the aging Datsun and follow the setting sun. Go west, young man, to the legendary land of multi-pitch climbs.

First stop, the fabled canyon of Eldorado: valley of endless sandstone, stomping grounds of Layton Kor, home of the Naked Edge. Our first night there, we walked the entire length of the road in gray drizzle, looking for the climbs. Nothing looked even remotely big enough to fit the visions of this place that our imaginations had conjured. We stood perplexed beneath a large outcrop that offered some shelter from the rain.

"Boy, Jim, this has got to be the place. The sign said ELDORADO SPRINGS. You don't suppose there might be more than one, do you?"

"No," he replied. "this must be it. We probably just didn't walk far enough up the canyon."

On the rock

Suddenly, a lone figure toting a chalk bag materialized out of the mists.

"Hey, buddy," we called. "where would we find the Bastille?"

He stared. "You're leaning against it."

Jim and I looked at each other and then slowly raised our heads to the rock wall above. "My God," Jim sighed, "it can't be more than two rope-lengths to the top." We stumbled back to camp feeling cheated.

Foreshortening is a nasty phenomenon, and we soon found out how wrong first impressions made on ignorant flatlanders in the pouring rain can be. A week later (most of which was spent backing off routes that were way over our heads) two enlightened, exhausted, and effectively humbled Minnesota climbers crept out of Colorado.

We coaxed our roadster north into the bleak and smooth, yet warmly familiar landscape of eastern Wyoming. We were headed for Devils Tower, and this time we would start right out giving the place the respect it deserved. We agreed to begin climbing 5.7 and then, if we were climbing well, maybe take a shot at some easier 5.8.

Soon the Tower loomed on the horizon, juxtaposed with the surrounding gentle hills like some great corrugated stump. Pulling into the cozy campground near its base, we noticed quite a few sites with mounds of ropes and climbing hardware heaped on the picnic tables. There were even some familiar "Land of 10,000 Lakes" license plates on the bumpers of the vehicles. A merry evening ensued in the company of a large group of fellow climbers. By and by the conversation wandered toward plans for tomorrow's climbing. The party atmosphere had loosened my tongue and apparently a few mental screws as well.

"Oh, I don't know," I drawled, "we were kind of thinking about doing something easy; 5.8-ish."

Jim's eyebrows shot up. "I wouldn't waste my time," someone offered. "Anything under 5.9 is usually pretty wide or dirty; 5.9 and above, though, now that's usually some pretty fine climbing. Say, didn't you fellows mention you were just in Eldorado?"

If I had, I sure hadn't meant to. That was the last thing I wanted to bring up. I resolved to stick to the subject, even though I really didn't like where that seemed to be leading either.

"5.9 and above huh? Well, ah, we've got to get used to the rock and stuff first." It sounded like the biggest dodge in the world, which, of course, it was.

"Nothing to get used to," the fellow persisted. "You can jam, can't you?"

"Oh, well . . . um . . . of course we can jam, but . . ."

"Well then, go for it!" He grinned. "You'll never find cleaner jamming than a Tower 5.10."

Jim's eyebrows had now disappeared above his hairline someplace. I needed a way out of this badly.

"What would you suggest for our first climb?" I asked, and cautiously added, "keeping in mind that we're still pretty wiped out from the long drive and would just as soon have sort of a rest day anyway."

"Do *Soler*. It's beautiful. Only two pitches and real easy. It's a great warm-up route."

Easy . . . warm-up . . . I liked the sound of that.

"Good protection?"

"The best. You can really lace it up."

My kind of climb.

"Well," I said. "*Soler*, huh? I think that sounds pretty good. Yup, that's what we'll do. *Soler*." Now that we were publicly committed, I asked, just as an afterthought, "So what's *Soler* rated anyway?"

"5.9 minus."

I had no idea where Jim's eyebrows were now, because his hand was over his face.

I'm not quite sure exactly how we got up *Soler*, whether it was luck, biorhythms, karma, or whatever. All I do know is that somehow, astonished but overjoyed, we found ourselves on top. By the time we reached the campground again, we had gotten a little cocky. I perused the guidebook.

"Okay, we've got four days left here . . . let's try this tomorrow (another 5.9 minus). If we get up that, we'll do this the next day (a solid 5.9), and if we can do that, we'll take a rest day and then do this: *Tulgey Wood*, 5.9 plus." Jim agreed. After all, it seemed quite a safe proposal because neither of us believed for a moment that we would ever get past day two of this scenario. And 5.9 plus? That was pure fantasy. We didn't think anymore about it as we concentrated on celebrating our newest conquest, and initiation into the world fringing on 5.9.

Thus, it was a bit disturbing when, two days later, we were still going strong. Our attempts on *Gooseberry Jam* and *Walt Bailey Memorial* ended with the same unlikely success as on *Soler*. Something was not right here and I attempted to reason it out. These climbs had been hard, but not at the absolute limit of our abilities like they should have been. Surely one of us should have fallen, at least once. I began to sense the hand of something or someone far greater than Jim or I in all of this. Somehow we were being led into a fateful rendezvous with the fourth day of our game plan. Then again, perhaps we had just been lucking out. I slept uneasily that night because now that I had to take it seriously, I had begun to fear *Tulgey Wood*.

We spent the first part of our rest day engaged in one of our favorite Devils Tower pastimes, "tourist baiting." We first discovered this game while hiking down the trail that circles the Tower, after climbing *Soler*. Fully clad in ropes and hardware, we were obviously quite a novelty to the countless tourists who also wander this path. Enthusiastically they questioned us about our climb, our gear, and the inevitable, "What's it like on top?" We laboriously answered their questions and then graciously offered to pose for photographs with their daughters.

It soon became apparent, however, that no matter how carefully and meticulously we described our activities, these people had absolutely no grasp of how rock climbing worked. We had run into this problem before, but Devils Tower vacationers seemed a breed apart. They had mastered the formidable skills necessary for piloting vehicles that were size, mass, and fuel consumption equivalents of the space shuttle, yet they were incapable of understanding even the most fundamental principles of roped climbing.

We soon tired of repeating our tedious and apparently fruitless explanations and began to make things up. The game quickly evolved. Whichever of us could tell the most outrageous lie about climbing the Tower and still be believed was considered the winner, and thus earned the prestigious and envied title of "Master-baiter." I currently held this honor for convincing an elderly couple from Ohio that the summit was littered with ruins and had, in fact, been the site of a Druid temple and observatory to which access had once been gained via an intricate network of cedar scaffolds and ladders.

This particular morning the game was not much fun, however. It was hard to have a light heart while standing in the shadow of *Tulgey Wood*.

Around noon we flopped down in the talus to watch a party from Montana who were engaged on the route. This was their second try. Their attempts on the previous day had climaxed with a nasty twenty-foot peel out of the crux on the first pitch. Now they had just reached the stance on top of the column that forms the short second pitch. We watched for over half an hour, and they didn't move. It was clear that they were both exhausted. We decided to leave for a while and run some errands. After driving the thirty miles to town and back, we returned to the talus. The two climbers were still on the ledge.

Later than evening, we ambled over to the Montana campsite with the intention of pumping them for some information. I was a little apprehensive and not at all sure that it was in the best of taste to bring up *Tulgey Wood* in light of the way that these guys had spent the past couple of days. It seemed a little like asking Mrs. Lincoln what she thought of the play. As it turned out, we should have stayed at home. For over an hour the "Big Sky" boys cussed and cursed and expounded on the terrors of *Tulgey Wood*. They had reached a point only about twenty feet above the spot where we had observed them before being once again, and this time conclusively, defeated. Psyched out, fed up, and all in, they backed down.

"I have absolutely nothing good to say about that route," one of them warned. "It's scary and sustained and a hell of a lot harder than any 5.9 that I've ever done."

His partner, though not much of a talker, seemed to agree. "It sucks," he muttered.

Jim and I had just about made up our minds to chicken out when a group of the local hard-men showed up. Before we could slip away, our more talkative host introduced us as "the Minnesota guys who are gonna have a crack at *Tulgey Wood* tomorrow . . . they gotta either be pretty good or pretty bold trying that bastard after watching us die on it."

"Balls," his partner grunted, "real balls." One of the locals gave us a crocodile smile. "*Tulgey Wood*, huh?" He grinned. "That's a real nice climb. Unique, that's for sure! Good luck, guys."

Something about the smirk on his face reminded me of the way Sitting Bull might have smiled at Custer the night before the massacre. Somehow, we had just gotten roped into doing another route that was way over our heads and that neither of us really wanted to do.

Back in our tent, we discussed our options. As I saw it, we had three choices: Quit climbing forever, change our names, or try the route. Jim liked climbing, and his name, but didn't want to do the route. Thus, he came up with another solution.

"You can lead the first two pitches," he said. "That's where the toughest stuff is, and it's your turn to lead the crux pitch anyway."

"Shouldn't we flip a coin or something?" I protested weakly.

"Now look," he continued, "it was your off-width mouth that got us into this mess in the first place. Besides, if we get an early start, we can probably back off in time to pack up and get a good head start on the drive home."

There is usually a clear boundary separating optimism from pessimism, but this skillful blending of the two left me somewhat confused in regard to his true disposition. My own bordered on despair.

And so shortly after sunrise on a beautiful August morning, when I could have been climbing any one of a dozen easier routes and really enjoying myself, I found myself tied to the front end of the rope, trussed up in enough clinking hardware to anchor a battleship, staring up at a climb that I knew would probably maim me for life. I turned to Jim. He was anchored securely to a little bush and was grinning, probably in anticipation of the bloodbath that was sure to follow. At that moment, he would have bet an orphan's crutch that he was never going to have to leave the ground.

"You know," I snapped, "if I crater, it's going to be on your conscience."

"No," he smiled, eyeing his position relative to the crack above, "I believe it'll be on my shoes."

I hoped that the shrub he was tied to was poison ivy.

The crack started out real nice. Fingers in, twist, toes on nubbins. The protection also seemed pretty reasonable.

Voices drifted across the talus from the visitors center. "Look, Martha! There's a man going up right there . . . no, lower . . . down near the bottom . . . climbing up that red rope." I winced.

The crack got smaller and entered a dihedral. "Boy, would this be a great spot for my #7 Taperlock (my favorite piece because of its pretty yellow cord), but it's still a long way to the top. I better save it till I really need it." I made do with a wired Stopper cammed sideways. Slowly I inched upward. Before long the crack became almost too thin to work my fingers into. Another little pocket appeared, perfect for the #7. The yellow cord tempted me, swinging back and forth on my rack like a hypnotist's watch, begging to be wedged into the bombproof groove. "No, my friend, I better save you for when it gets really desperate up above." I rigged another imaginative wired placement and continued on.

The crack had all but sealed up by the time I reached an awkward rest stance right below the crux. I looked up and saw ten feet of bulging dihedral with no crack. I slipped a #2 wired Stopper into the seam and recalled that my last two pieces had also been pretty marginal. I despaired at my frugality with my precious #7 and vowed that if I lived through this, I would mercilessly hammer that damned Taperlock into tinfoil. I thought once more of Jim, grinning and safe and laced to that plant. I yanked hard on the #2, sealing it deep inside the seam. With any luck, he'd have one hell of a time trying to get it out.

I hooked my fingertips up and onto some very obscure holds on the right wall, planted my feet on the left, and began to lieback. With the intense effort the surrounding world faded out of my perception and was replaced with a universe consisting of the two feet of rock surrounding my face and the magnified tom-toms of my racing heartbeat. My skull became a vacuous container rocking with the echoes of fragmented voices and imaginary noises:

"Cigarette or a blindfold?"

(a siren began to wail)

"Our Father, who art in heaven . . ."

(warning buzzers)

"Impact force equals mass times the acceleration of gravity."

(Pop! And the second stopper below spun lazily earthward)

"Next, please."

(bells tolling)

". . . Thy kingdom come, Thy will be done . . ."

(weeping)

"Ashes to ashes . . ."

(bugle *Taps*)

"So young . . ."

(snapping perlon)

"so much to live for."

(twisting aluminum)

Suddenly my hand was on a jug. My feet were on a small ledge. I was confused. I looked down, and the hellish dihedral bulged out below. I looked up, and a ladder of cracks and knobs led ten feet to a belay stance. Slowly it dawned on me.

"I did it. My God, I did it!" And yet something was wrong. I felt dizzy and began to see spots. Only as my head began to spin did I fully realize what the problem was. I wasn't breathing! Judging by the ringing in my ears, I had probably been holding my breath through the entire crux.

I rapidly reinflated my lungs with gluttonous gasps. Fully conscious again, I hastily reconciled with my #7 and popped it into a slot; my first good piece in miles. A quick scramble and I was at the belay, where I let out a whoop so unique in tone and intensity that the tourists below fled eagerly to the telescopes in the hopes of spotting either a spectacular injury or a dangling corpse. After making myself secure, I sat back against the wall and relished the level ledge. I closed my eyes and smiled.

An impatient tug on the rope reminded me that Jim had yet to undergo the ordeal. As I took in the slack, I yelled words of advice and encouragement. Secretly, of course, I hoped he would find it a bitch. I leaned out of my perch to watch him make his preparations to follow. I chuckled with uncontrollable delight when at last he removed the sling between himself and the bush, thus severing his last tenuous connection with the horizontal. I slumped back onto the ledge when at last he began to climb, as I much preferred imagining him pawing and thrashing to watching him dance up in a style that would rob me of my hard-earned feelings of superhuman ability. By the time he reached the crux, however, the rope was coming in unusually slow, and I began to hear vague curses amidst remarkably labored breathing. By God, old Jim really was having trouble!

It never crossed my mind that he was a good foot shorter than myself, and that the crux holds had been just within my reach. I had also temporarily forgotten about the wired stopper that I had bitterly jammed deep within the hairline crack. And it didn't occur to me that Jim's ravaged hands were stiffly bound with more tape than Tutankhamun's. Consequently, I interpreted each grunt and gasp as a genuine compliment of my fine lead.

When he finally heaved himself onto the stance, I quickly stripped him of the gear he had cleaned and announced that I was ready to tackle the second pitch.

Actually, it wasn't much of a pitch at all. Approximately twenty feet long, it appeared to consist of four identical moves of 5.9-ish liebacking. By standing on tiptoe I could place a nut almost halfway up the pitch, and so it was also well protected.

All that was in my mind, however, was that this would be my last hard lead and that it was rated easier and was infinitely shorter than the pitch I had just finished. The crux was below us and to me, deluded by my success, this pitch looked trivial. To Jim it meant everything. It represented his last chance and hope that I might fail and he might be spared the opportunity of leading the only remaining crux of the climb: the endless third pitch.

I was determined, however, that any failure on this route would not be mine. After all, I reasoned, hadn't I just led the crux pitch without a fall? Furthermore, hadn't I done the hardest climbing without oxygen? (The difference between gasping above eight thousand meters on a Himalayan peak and holding your breath out of terror on a prairie rock climb did not seem significant as my ego blossomed.) And wasn't I now embarking on my second consecutive 5.9 or harder lead in order that my second might rest himself for one paltry pitch of less or equal rating? The fact that his pitch would be longer than all of mine combined also escaped me in my slightly "touched" state of mind. I believe psychologists call this "delusions of grandeur." It is an accurate term, for at this point I had become mentally equivalent to the greatest alpinist on earth.

I seized the crack with iron fingers, and with a lusty roar I informed a pale Jim that "this shouldn't take long, it's only 5.9!" I leapt catlike onto the unsuspecting dihedral, where after two feet of upward progress, attained by some impressively overdone moves exhibiting classical liebacking techniques, I slid with a thump back down onto the ledge.

The fog in my brain began to clear. I was not the world's greatest climber, either mentally or obviously physically. I was, in fact, a mediocre toproping specialist from an area known geographically as the Great Plains. I further realized that I was damn lucky that I had gotten up what I had so far, but I optimistically reasoned that what I had done once I ought to be able to repeat.

I decided that the key to a pitch this short was momentum. I knew I would have to discard the textbook techniques for my own more comfortable and effective personal style.

My method of climbing is based on a little known principle of physics called the Sub-linear Vector Axiom. It is basically an inversion of all the known laws pertaining to the conservation of energy. Reduced to its simplest form it states, "A climber in motion tends to seek rest." How Newton missed this one is a real mystery. In practice it involves an initial output of massive quantities of energy. As the supply is rapidly depleted, a sort of coasting effect takes over that will hopefully carry you to some kind of ledge. If not, you're screwed. Less educated climbers, upon observing this technique, often remark that it looks suspiciously similar to uncontrolled thrashing and lunging. This is the price I pay for introducing high-powered science into the relatively Neanderthal world of athletics.

I launched myself off the belay ledge, alternately swimming and clawing my way upward. My initial surge gained me an almost instant ten feet. Inertia propelled me another five. Sure enough, a rest stance appeared just as gravity decided that this had gone on long enough. My #7 dived deeply into the bowels of the crack. You could have hung a truck on that placement, and I didn't even flinch at using up the piece. I'd be damned if I'd make the same mistake two pitches in a row.

Looking up, I was confronted with a bulging rounded slab. It appeared to be the last obstacle before the belay, and Jim was going to get his pitch because the anticipation of success had triggered a mental relapse and I had become Reinhold Messner again. I humped my way upward and was soon confronting bolts, old runners, and a ledge you could roller-skate on.

I was exuberant and built a delirious belay. "Let's hear it for good anchors! Three cheers for a safe and comfortable stance: Clip-clip-hooray!" Finally, lashed to enough points to moor the USS *Nimitz*, I sat down and reeled in my little fish. When at last he arrived, Jim was pretty bummed out and not just a little scared.

"Well, James, the ball is in your court now." Nothing like rubbing a little salt in an open wound, I always say.

He eyed my belay setup. Unceremoniously, he began to dismantle it, mumbling something about needing chockstones. The pieces were all finger size, and his pitch was all fist and off-width, but I was still anchored to bolts and so I allowed him this small retribution. I draped him with the rack, and the baton was passed.

When God built Devils Tower, He smiled graciously upon rock climbers. When He chiseled out the third pitch of *Tugley Wood*, He was either in a hurry, a particularly unpleasant mood, or making a very bad joke. A single wide crack runs its entire length. Though the first pitch is the technical crux of the route, the third pitch is vastly more difficult physically. The first pitch has many reasonable rest positions, and the real difficult section is brief. The third pitch is moderately hard but incredibly sustained, almost impossible to rest on, and hard to protect. It certainly represents as great a barrier to successfully completing the route as the first pitch.

Of course, at this point we knew little or none of this. Certainly Jim was closer to guessing the truth than I was, because after eyeing it for a few minutes and tentatively feeling out the first ten feet, he suddenly sagged back onto the one and only nut that he had placed and said, "No."

Still basking in the glory of my performance, this caught me quite off guard. "What?"

"No," he repeated.

"What do you mean 'no'?" I demanded.

"No," he shouted. "N-O. It's a short adverb used to communicate denial, refusal, or dissent, and in this particular case it means all three. Basically, what it boils down to is that I don't think I want to do this."

Well, if this didn't beat all. And after I had gotten us so far! Through the crux (or so I thought), without a fall (an event as unlikely as the repayment of the French war debt), and without ever once considering the possibility of retreat (this, I believe, marks the point where I finally lost all touch with reality). What's wrong with him anyway, the sissy! What kind of an attitude is that, saying "no" and just giving up? Who does he think he is, uttering negatives while dangling so close above the belay that if I only had a bat I could reach up and smash his spine except that he doesn't seem to have one.

I leaped to my feet, shook my fist, and roared. "Now listen here! I upheld my half of the bargain! I climbed my ass off to get us to this point, and now that we're almost there and past the hardest part and have one crummy 5.9 pitch left to go, nobody in this party is going to hang up here and shout 'No!'"

"Do you want to lead it?" Jim asked.

"No!" I shouted.

We were in a fix. I knew Jim was capable of climbing this thing, but a climber in the grips of a psych-out is as hard to budge as mercury in a Duluth winter. I quickly realized that the key to resolving this crisis did not lie on physical threats. Jim, although considerably shorter, could undoubtedly mash me to a pulp at will. Nor was the answer to be found through verbal abuse, for Jim could not be menaced for the same reason. Psychology seemed a safer and more logical alternative.

I resolved to subtly prod him with guilt by reminding him of the sense of duty that partners have to each other, and of the trust and faith that we place in each other when we bond ourselves with perlon. The relationship is unique to climbers and trapeze artists, but we don't use nets. Yes, friends are special, and climbing partners are special among friends. Jim would see this and realize that he owed me his best shot.

"Jim?"

"Yeah?"

"I've always been proud to call you my climbing partner. And I want you to know that, well, if you're not feeling well we can rap off right now and, heck, it won't change a thing . . . old buddy."

"Stuff it, Dave, it's not going to work."

So much for Plan A. Plan B involved playing on his ego. I figured I could caress it to the point where his head would swell as big as a balloon and he would float right up the crack.

"Jim?"

"Yeah?"

"I don't know if I've ever told you this, but I've always admired the style and fortitude you exhibit when you climb. It's damn impressive. You are one tiger. Grrr."

"Thanks. Dave. You want to lower me back down to the stance now?"

I was rapidly running out of cards to play. One avenue remained with which to compel him, but the result if it failed was even more unthinkable than simply backing off the route. I hesitated for long moments, but at last, a true gambler at heart, I elected to pursue it.

"Say, Jim?"

"Yeah?"

"If you're still willing, I think maybe I would like to take a crack at this thing. Why don't we switch places?"

He was climbing!

Once he got under way, he never even looked back. He looked like one of those machines they use to hammer in railroad spikes: chugging along at full steam and then, bam! in goes a piece of metal and then chug on again to the next one. He never even really broke stride. Every foot of rope that fed out raised my spirits one full notch. We were actually going to do it! I leaned back, relaxed, and smiled.

I was still smiling when I noticed that Jim was out of rope. The guidebook said 160 feet for this pitch, so Jim must be there. I looked up. Either the guidebook or the people who made my rope lied, because he was still below the overhang at the top of the pitch, and that meant at least ten feet left to go.

The rope was now taut between us, and from high above came a faint stream of seemingly meaningless babble: "More . . . wrote . . . you . . . trick!" I deduced from this that Jim was near his wits' end and firmly gripped in the iron hand of panic. But then I considered that that didn't seem like Jim at all . . . which led me to a simpler truth: The wind and distance were making all of his *p*'s sound like *t*'s.

Thus it was that in less than ten seconds time, I left the world of supine bliss and total relaxation and was returned to the vertical struggle unwilling, unprepared, and relatively unbelayed. Daydreaming one minute, nightmare the next. I thrashed up ten feet, but the alarming loop of rope that dangled below cautioned me to slow down and let Jim catch up. In order to at least create the illusion of a good belay, I was going to have to match his pace. Why wasn't he moving? I glanced up. Miles above, Jim was coming to grips with the final overhang. Slowly the loop of rope below me inched up. I tried to preoccupy myself with prying loose the big hex he had hung on. At last the rope drew tight again and I moved on.

The crack was getting wider, and in order to jam, my arm was crammed in up to the shoulder. Soon the good jams receded even deeper, and just as I gave them up and slipped out and into a much more strenuous and infinitely less secure lieback, I received a long-distance call from Jim: "Off belay."

Now, rationally I should have realized that he was the one who was now "off belay," but rational isn't exactly the word I would choose to best describe my state of mind at that particular moment. After all, if you were right in the middle of some pretty desperate moves, and the guy at the other end of the rope suddenly yelled "off belay," whose neck would you assume was on the chopping block?

Pulling up and in again, I managed to stuff both feet into the crack. Side by side they just spanned its width, but I knew that it was one of those situations where taking too much weight off my arms might cause my feet to pop through, and this dark crack would drop me like a gallows. The difference would be that here, there might not be a sudden tightening of the rope before I slapped the pavement. I was just aiming my jump for the belay ledge when Jim called back: "Belay on." I realized then that the only danger in my falling was the possibility of jerking Jim off his stance before he got any anchors in. As it turned out, this would have been unlikely because his belay ledge was so huge that you could have played golf on it.

The really awkward off-width only lasted thirty feet or so, and then the crack closed back up a little. This was fine for the moment, but there was still at least 120 feet of fist jams capped by an overhang left to go. Very few details of the rest of the pitch stick in my memory, for indeed, each ten feet seemed a carbon copy of the ten feet before. Also, I can't be 100 percent sure that I was conscious the whole time.

A general impression does remain, however. Physically it was a lot like running a marathon with a pillow tied around my face. Mentally, it was incredibly dulling—like staring at checkered wallpaper. I remember almost falling a lot, but I do that on every climb. I was particularly impressed by the quantity and quality of Jim's protection. There was very little and it was very poor—just a few big hexentrics seeming to defy gravity in the parallel-sided crack and some large Titons cammed into place only under the weight of their own slings.

When at last I found myself plastered under the final overhang, my needle was on empty. I was grateful to be free of the fist-crack treadmill but was unsure if I could cope with this last obstacle. My brain was a sponge in an ocean of adrenaline, and it was clear that this chemical was the only fuel that remained with which to propel me in the direction I needed to go. With every muscle fiber and neuron firing sparks of protest, I reached up, jammed, pulled, and kicked. And then again, and again, until I flopped like some great beached tuna onto Jim and the eighteenth green.

We spent a great deal of time recuperating on that ledge before we felt able to move on. The remaining two pitches seemed quite trivial in light of what we had just done. They consisted mainly of stemming blocky and weathered chimneys that were choked and spattered with guano and quite typical of the upper part of many of the routes at Devils Tower. The only move that was at all memorable was actually pulling onto the belay ledge at the end of the fourth pitch. The technique required seemed awfully similar to that used when getting into a top bunk without a ladder.

At any rate, we flashed these pitches running on a rich mixture of euphoria and adrenaline. At long last, and in defiance of all the known laws of probability, we stood on top of *Tulgey Wood*. Jim and I raced and danced through the summit prairie, and life was never so good.

I marveled at the transition we had made this day, finally smashing through the formidable barrier beyond 5.8. We had done a multi-pitch route, consistently climbing 5.9 or harder, and without a fall. We would not be eating quiche this night.

With great pride we carefully and legibly printed our names and the route title in the summit register. Then we zipped down the four rappels to the base of the tower at speeds that left our friction gear sizzling and popping as we spat to cool them down.

As we trudged the footpath back around the Tower toward our car, I felt a great need to express the deep and moving feelings I was experiencing from our adventure. I wanted to communicate to Jim my personal joy in our achievement and thank him for his role in it as partner and friend. I had to make sure that he was sharing my delight at our triumph.

And so, as we walked the narrow trail, myself in front and Jim at my heels, I made a speech. The exact text is not important, but let us simply say that for me it seemed quite eloquent. I told him that this had been one of the greatest days of my life, certainly of my climbing career. I said things that climbers rarely share after the route is done, like how petrified I had been on my leads and how impressed I had been by his. I confessed the emotions I had felt on the route, feelings that all climbers have but that even the closest part-ners usually keep hidden. Things like envy and jealousy of the other's skills, or delight when the other slips where you didn't, and disappointment when they don't where you had trouble. I admitted that the statements I had made in my ruse to get him moving on the third pitch had, in fact, been true, except for the one that had finally worked.

When I finished, I waited for some word in answer, but there was only silence. Surely after such a baring of my soul the least he could do was reciprocate just a little. Hadn't he heard a word I had said? I turned and discovered that he hadn't.

Jim was about two hundred feet back, near the telescopes. He was engaged in vigorous conversation with a man in baggy khaki pants who was harnessed to the world's largest Nikon. I ambled back a little until I could make out his familiar voice.

"That's right, hollow. The thing's as hollow as a rotten log! And filled with rainwater . . . there's a lake on top. That's why we don't hammer in spikes here like you see them do on TV. The Park Service is afraid we'll bang 'em in too deep and drain the damn thing!"

I smiled and turned and clanked back down toward the parking lot in search of my own tourist to play with.

FIRST TO CLIMB LIZARD HEAD
(1921)
Albert L. Ellingwood

A million years ago, in the region men were to call the Silvery San Juan, the granite foundations of the earth were riven and from the fissures bubbling lava welled forth in a mighty flood. Engulfing all things living in its destructive progress, it spread far and wide over canyon, stream, and mountain, and when it had spent its force, its sluggish verge enclosed a desolate area so large the king of birds could hardly circle it from dawn to dusk.

It would be in vain to ask how great the multitude of monsters overwhelmed beneath the sticky mud. Only the greatest of them all, the ancient ancestor of the puny Titanosaurs of a much later age, left even a trace behind. Isolated on an outstanding ridge and slowly swallowed up in the inexorable ooze, he struggled despairingly, even when altogether submerged. At last convulsion brought to the already hardening surface only his enormous horn thickly coated with the viscid fluid. All became rock in time, and of the life before the cataclysm there was no witness but this huge monocerous monument.

Millenniums file by and the waste places are redeemed. Seismic upheavals shatter the great plateau, erosion and disintegration play a potent part, forests and rivers appear and

Lizard Head

make a new world to welcome the fauna of a new age. Men come at last—men who fill the valleys with fields of grain, torture the bowels of the earth in search for precious metals, spread towns in mountain parks, and cast a tenuous path of steel across the mountain ranges. But ever the towering monolith defies them, keeping its lofty heights unsoiled by human touch.

"Lizard Head . . . is a column with nearly vertical walls on all sides, rising nearly three hundred feet above its platform. Its summit is inaccessible, and the reason for its preservation is not evident. At the base it is a bedded mass of andesitic breccia . . . and a horizontal banding is visible far up on its walls, although a vertical fissuring renders this obscure in many places. It is possible that there is here a rounded or oval neck of massive rock . . . which has indurated the surrounding tuffs, so that the core is concealed by a shell of this character."

This curious rocky "head" is an outcropping at the highest possible point of a long semicircular ridge that forms the eastern portion of the Mount Wilson group. Geologically this majestic group is but an offshoot or outlier of the San Juan Mountains, but like several other spurs in the Colorado Rockies, it surpasses the main range in ruggedness and alpine dignity and beauty.

Besides the unique Lizard Head, with which we are here concerned, it contains (to mention only the highest peaks) Gladstone Peak (over 13,800 feet), Wilson Peak (14,026 feet), and Mount Wilson itself (14,250 feet); the last is the fourteenth peak in a state that boasts forty-two peaks over fourteen thousand feet in height and (to quote from a forest service scribe) "offers a difficult and in part a dangerous climb, but affords one of the most beautiful views obtainable in the southern part of the state."

The group as a whole is isolated from the mass of the volcanic complex of the San Juan region by the deep erosion of the San Miguel River, which flows northward into the Gunnison, and the Rio Dolores, which flows in the opposite direction.

The government geologist had said the Lizard Head was inaccessible, and the forest service pamphlet corroborated him: "The sheer rock face of Lizard Head Peak (13,156 feet) has never yet been climbed by man."

The forest supervisor at Durango wrote in response to my inquiry: "It is my understanding that the Lizard Head has never been scaled." Finally, after taking three weeks to get "reliable information," Mr. Richard R. Thompson, the forest ranger at Rico (which is the nearest ranger station to the Lizard Head), replied: "It is said that Lizard Head has never been climbed, and I believe that it is unclimbable from either face." "Inaccessible" and "unclimbable" are strong words and are like a red flag to the enthusiastic alpinist; so when, with Barton Hoag of Colorado Springs, I planned three weeks of camping and climbing in the San Juan, it is hardly necessary to say the Lizard Head was an objective.

From our first peak, the Uncompahgre, loftiest of the San Juan region (14,306 feet), we sought it eagerly with our powerful glasses, and picking it out with difficulty in the early morning mist across thirty-five miles of the most tangled confusion of mountains in Colorado, let our eyes rest long upon it, in earnest anticipation of what it held in store for us. We had several glimpses of it as we gradually worked closer, from the highest summits of the Lake Fork section of the San Juan proper and from the Needle Mountains south of Silverton. Finally, from the favored summit of Mount Sneffles (the finest view in the San Juan), we gazed admiringly upon the slender shaft of rock only fifteen miles away and wondered if we were destined to stand upon its top.

Our course lay southwest along the sheep driveway for a mile and a half and then turned off on a trail to the right, which brought us to Slate Creek for lunch, for we had not got started till 11:10. So far there was practically no climbing, but now the trail swung to the north and headed for the saddle (11,800 feet) between Gladstone and the Lizard Head, and in the next four and a half miles there is an ascent of sixteen hundred feet. Relaying the packs to the top of the pass, we dropped down rapidly to the tree line in the east branch of Bilk Basin and pitched camp at about 11,300 feet.

This is undoubtedly the best base of operations. It is at the very foot of the Lizard Head ridge and only fifteen hundred feet below the platform upon which the great rock rests. It can be reached by trail, either from the Lizard Head station as we came (about eight and a half miles) or from the railway crossing opposite the Belt ranch in the San Miguel valley.

The latter route climbs over the north shoulder of Sunshine Mountain and ascends Bilk Creek; it is shorter than the route we took by perhaps two miles but involves a climb of twenty-six hundred feet instead of sixteen hundred, and the long stretch in the valley below the camp is very steep indeed for heavy packs. One would have to go a considerable distance from the trail to find both wood and water to the southwest of the Head, and there is no trail at all up Wilson Creek to the east.

The camp in Bilk Basin is also favorably situated for attacking Wilson Peak, Gladstone, and Mount Wilson. It would be difficult to find a more beautiful site. Pitched on the high east bank of a roaring creek, it looks out from the shelter of tall Engelmanns upon the thick green spruce carpet of the lower basin, from which the long brown slope of Wilson Peak stretches impressively into the western sky. Farther to the left stands Gladstone's rocky cone, the jagged eastern ridge of which cuts off from view the snowy heights of Mount Wilson.

For two days we kept close to our tarp lean-to, forced to remain inactive by the unkind weather. The morning of the third was cloudy, but it started to clear after breakfast, and, resolved to let no opportunity escape, we hurriedly packed a lunch and set out for the ridge. An Indian boy who was herding fifteen hundred sheep over in the West Basin had dropped in for a chat after breakfast, and we told him as we packed that we were going to climb the Lizard Head. He evidently thought we were "ragging" him and was highly amused. If he had believed we were seriously planning such an attempt, doubtless he would have set us down as lunatics.

It sits astride the narrow ridge, in outline very like a rough, Cyclopean arrowhead with shallow notch and somewhat shattered tip. The picture taken from this point shows all of the west face and part of the east as well, for the rock narrows to the north, and the photograph is taken from west of north. Consequently the base appears thicker than it is.

Nor is the apparent height the true one; for, as can be seen from other pictures, the summit is distinctly farther from an observer on this ridge than is the base. According to the geologist quoted above, the top is practically three hundred feet above the ridge. The USGS map would make it nearer 450, and a calculation made by the writer from observations taken on the ridge gives 350 as the height. The last figure is a minimum if one may judge by the ascent, on which our one-hundred-foot alpine rope made a very good tape measure.

The rock is almost as long as it is high but probably does not exceed 125 feet in thickness at any point. Only when seen from either side (necessarily from a distance) does it to any degree justify its name, and the writer must confess that even then he thinks its resemblance to a saurian's head not over-strong. A striking feature easily seen in the ridge picture and those taken from the west is the slender pinnacle that springs from a small ledge below and to the northwest of the summit; the "Finger" we called it, and it seemed raised in warning as we went along the ridge.

It was apparent when we reached the Head that there was nasty work before us. A rottener mass of rock is inconceivable. The core may still be solid, but the "surrounding tuffs" are seeking a lower level in large quantities. This far-advanced disintegration was our greatest obstacle. Absolutely the whole surface of the rock is loose, and pebbles rain down from the sides as readily as needles from an aging Christmas tree.

In many places one could with one hand pull down hundreds of pounds of fragments, and occasionally we could hear the crashing of small avalanches that fell without human prompting. In some parts of the San Juan we had run across the rumor that the Lizard Head or a large part thereof had fallen off a year or two ago; but though the ridge is covered with the detritus of the ages, there is no evidence of a recent catastrophe of any magnitude. However, it is more than probable that large masses plunge down to the long talus slopes from time to time.

We saw at a glance that the east face was out of the question; it is an almost sheer drop from near the summit of the Head to far below the level of the ridge on which we stood. And the north edge was nearly as impossible—its inclination measured eighty-five degrees. Working along the western side we reached the other end, which is so broad it might be called a face. A peek around the southeast corner confirmed us in our opinion that the east face will not be climbed till man has learned how to defy the law of gravity.

There were a couple of spots along the west face that seemed worth trying as a last resort, but from below they looked like rather a forlorn hope, and after our later experience on the rock it was clear that there would have been little chance of success by any such route. Seen from the pass to the west three days before, the south end had appeared to be the most feasible line of attack, but a closer inspection showed that there were no holds for more than a few feet, except in a couple of cracks near the southwest corner. We roped up and I tried them both, getting perhaps seventy-five feet in the first and hardly twenty-five feet in the second when forced to retreat.

Then we went around the corner and tried the first promising crack on the west side. This proved the beginning of a feasible route, so I will try to describe it carefully, following my diary notes quite closely. It was about 12:00 when I began this third attack. Hoag sought shelter around the corner, for each movement that I made sent down a rattling shower of stones. Needless to say, every hand- and foothold had to be tested with the utmost thoroughness. Most of the enticing small holds crumbled at a touch, and large masses of the loosely compacted pebbles would topple dangerously at a slight pull.

As we topped the ridge the north end of the massive rock burst full upon us with startling suddenness. The first fifteen or twenty feet was a rather open stretch, practically vertical and with exiguous holds about the size of a thimble that at once forced me to put off my leather gloves. When rock is treacherous and small firm holds are scarce—and important— even fingernails may be of use. But soon the crack deepened and narrowed, and resorting to the back-and-knee method I felt much more secure. This cross-bracing became easier as I ascended, but I sought in vain a secure place to wait for my companion to come up to me.

Grateful indeed I was for the extra length of this rope that had been obtained originally for four-party climbing. With the eighty-foot rope that is recommended by Abraham, the great English alpinist, I should have been forced to await Hoag in a very wearying cross-braced position, and after he had reached me he would have had to take the same position and protect himself as best he could from the unavoidable hail of stone caused by my further ascent.

At ninety feet I climbed out on a small ledge to the right and found fair standing and two reassuring handholds, but, alas! no belaying-pin. Working upwards and into the crack again I went on, pulling Hoag from his shelter to give a few feet more, until, literally at the end of my rope, I found an anchor, safe and secure though rather awkward for the operator. With one foot on a ledge three inches wide and seven or eight inches long, the other swinging in midair, the right hand hooked over a small sharp rock at arm's length overhead and the left free to manipulate the rope over a small point about shoulder high, I called, "Come on."

The first steep pitch gave a good deal of trouble, as it had to me, but once in the crack, Hoag soon reached the ninety-foot ledge and prepared to make himself comfortable. This first one-hundred-foot section averaged about eighty degrees in inclination, and the lowest pitch and one just under the Hoag ledge were practically perpendicular.

Above me the main crack was quite impossible, and the nose upon the right no less so. A small crack, hardly large enough to thrust one's hand in, branched off to the left across a more open stretch of rock discouragingly steep and smooth. Hoag, who was carrying the rucksack, tied three spikes into the rope and I pulled them up—long, thick spikes, somewhat like those used for steps on telegraph poles. Driving one in the crack about waist high to step upon, I squirmed my way up an eight-foot wall where even the slight friction of my clothes on the almost vertical rock was welcome aid, for there were handholds only for the fingertips.

An easier slope succeeded this, but twenty feet farther on there was another pitch that went straight up and ended in a slightly overhanging brow. This delayed progress for some time, but with the aid of another spike and a long cross-brace that stretched me to the limit, I finally pulled over and to my great relief found myself on an easier grade (probably about seventy-five degrees). The temptation was to hurry, but the loose rock was especially treacherous and I restrained myself.

At the head of this stretch and once again at the end of my rope, I reached a little platform roughly three feet wide and five feet long and fairly level. A fine anchor rock stood two feet high at its edge, and belaying the rope around this, I called for Hoag to join me. It was a chilly wait, for my second *bonne bouche* gave him quite a bit of trouble with its scarcity of holds and the embarrassing brow that called for very delicate adjustment of one's balance in midair; and I had plenty of time to realize he must have well nigh congealed on his narrow ledge while I was struggling with these difficulties for the first time.

This was his introduction to prime rock climbing, and I was more than pleased with his patience, skill, and caution. He reached the anchorage in fine fettle, and we pushed on at once.

A six-foot wall confronted us. Easily but gingerly we climbed around and up over its right nose and found ourselves on a large shelf sloping to the south at perhaps thirty degrees and cut into north and south by a couple of narrow rock gullies that evidently led to cracks on the south end of the Head. Carefully we worked to the left, gaining about fifty feet in altitude before coming up against the sheer, smooth cliff at the head of the shelf. It looked decidedly dubious at first. There were cracks higher up on the wall, but they all ran out eight or ten feet above the base.

Any route would be slow at best, and we could not see what impossibilities awaited us at the top. The summit of the Head was somewhere to the north—but how far and how much higher and behind what barricades? These were pertinent questions, for the afternoon was waning rapidly.

Finally I decided to try to reach a crack that lay near the south end of the wall and appeared to lead through to the arête above. The first eight or nine feet was an overhanging pocket or alcove, and above this the wall was vertical and unbroken save for the narrow end of the crack to which we aspired. It was a difficult problem—one of the four real pièces de résistance of the whole climb.

Standing on Hoag's shoulders, I proved all things within reach for what must have seemed an interminable time to him. At last I found holds at arm's length, but it was a strenuous pull to reach the crack. Equally strenuous it was, though not difficult technically, to wriggle up the narrow cleft with a very crowded back-and-knee cross-brace. This was the safest stretch of the day, and the hardest physical work.

At the extreme limit of the rope I reached a large, safe anchor rock at the south end of the summit arête and saw that we had won. Shouting down the glad tidings, I told Hoag to come on. He had no shoulders to support him but a rope above, and after he was over the alcove all went well.

From this last anchor rock there is an easy ascent northwards along a fairly sharp ridge of loose rock, across a small gap where one gets a sensational view down the sheer east cliffs, and finally a careful climb over a few large rocks to the top, which is perhaps fifty feet above the anchor rock. The situation was not without its thrills. The actual summit is quite small, and the rocks are ready to slide off on every side. There was no sign that anyone had been before us.

We built a cairn as large as we could find support for, and placed at its foot a Prince Albert tobacco can containing a slip of paper with the usual data. Unfortunately the terrain did not permit a good picture of the top, but each of us snapped the other precariously balanced near the cairn.

The sun was too low by this time to expect good results, but we tried to get some photographic record of the intricate jumble of mountains along the eastern skyline and of the magnificent Wilson group to the west. The lonesome Lizard

Head is an ideal position for both views. Also we got a spectacular close-up of the fifteen-foot Finger, which looked as if it were so far gone that the slightest push would topple it from its resting place.

We agreed that a million dollars would not tempt us to its top—for riches are of this world, not the next. Incidentally, it would be a painstaking feat to reach its base.

We had arrived at 4:25, and a half hour escaped before we could bring ourselves to leave. The return route was the same, for we had no time to waste on very dubious experiments. Hoag made good speed down the first crack. I drove in a spike and looped the rope around it to secure me for the first few feet, then shook it off, wriggled down easily to the alcove, and jumped.

The second hundred was our bête noire. Hoag went down to his old ledge, leaning heavily on the rope and moving an inch at a time down the two spiked walls. There he untied the rope and prepared for as comfortable a sojourn as possible.

Looping the rope at its middle around the big anchor rock, I went down to the first spike, grateful indeed for the rope when I dropped over the projecting brow. It was a ticklish task to get past this *mauvais pas*, and I wondered again and again how I had ever ascended it without a rope, being quite certain I would not come down it ropeless for a good deal. My plan was to pull the loose end of the rope around the rock, loop it again over the spike to which I now clung, and then drop on down to the first anchor of the day.

But, alas, the rope would not come. I shook it violently to loosen it—and something else came. A stone as large as my fist suddenly shot off the brow and landed squarely on the top of my head. I have a thick head of hair, and fortunately, contrary to my usual practice, I was wearing a heavy hat. Even so, the scalp was broken (as I found later), and I was nearly knocked from my very insecure position. I felt light-headed and tied closely to the spike for a few minutes, to make sure that I could find myself when wanted.

Hoag had suffered too; a small rock ricochetted and, travelling at good speed, smote him on the back of the head as he bowed to protect his face against the flying pebbles. Luckily he was well braced on the ledge, and his hands were clenched and cramped over good holds. But it was a close shave, for he saw many stars and carried a bump like a large walnut for several days to come.

Worst of all, the rope could not be budged. I climbed up, readjusted it and tried again, but to no purpose. It was not jammed, but there was enough friction on the rough surface of the big rock and on the slope and brow to resist all the pull I could exert. Up again I went and reconnoitered. There was no other possible anchor. I scouted the gullies leading to the south-end cracks—to no avail.

Hoag and I held a long-distance consultation. I made one more round-trip and profited nothing. It was enough; the rope must go the way of so many ropes on Chamonix aiguilles. I tied the end to the stubborn anchor and went down to my old ledge near Hoag. He used the last few feet to steady him into the crack, let go, and worked slowly toward the ground.

The last pitch balked him for some time. The small holds that had assisted us up were undiscoverable. Suddenly he slipped and, leaving a section of his pants behind, drifted relentlessly downward till the wall became vertical and then jumped (perhaps fifteen feet) to the rocks below. I followed with more caution, regretfully saying good-bye to the rope that had served me for five good seasons.

All went well till the holds got scarce. It was too dark now to see what was below me on the cliff, and I did not care to risk a jump and possibly a sprained ankle unless I had to. So I let down a long string for the folding lantern that we had left behind at noontide, and by its light slowly picked my way down to the ground.

It was a quarter to nine, and the sandwiches and raisins from the second rucksack were as good as a five-course dinner at the Ritz. There was a bright moon now, just at the full, and, once out of the Head's huge shadow, we had easy going over the talus slopes and snow-filled ravines to camp. Getting a hot supper and exchanging gratified reminiscences of the climb brought midnight before we sought our blankets.

Our Indian friend dropped in next morning as we were setting out for Wilson Peak and Mount Wilson, and we told him we had stood upon Lizard Head. He grinned as pleasantly and as incredulously as ever. It was still a good joke, anyway.

NEW YORK STORIES: BOULDERING IN THE BIG APPLE AND BEYOND (1999)

Josh Lowell

New York has taught me everything I know about bouldering. Here's what I know.

I. Every boulder problem begins in the mind. *The most compelling boulder in the world is merely a chunk of rock until someone notices it, imagines a path of human motion over its surface, and makes the critical leap of actually trying it. Putting on shoes, taping down fingers, chalking up hands, and thrashing the body in the blind hope that something inspiring will reveal itself in the process. If you are a boulderer, if difficult movement on rock is your passion, you will find inspiration each time you open your eyes.*

I admit that I was doubtful when Ivan began raving to me about the incredible bouldering in the Gunks. I was living back on the East Coast for the first time in five years, spending the winter working in a gym between fall and spring road trips. At the competitions that year, the talk in iso was always the same, and it was always coming from the prolific mouth of Ivan Greene.

The smallest challenges are often as hard as the biggest

"Dude, the shit is rid*iiiiiiiii*culous, yo! There's *soooo* many fat problems, and *maaaad* hard, too. Full-on potential, *un*tapped. I'm telling you bro, it's the bomb!"

Ivan has the energy of three people stuffed into a frame too small to contain it. His chest and arms bulge obscenely, as if his intensity might burst through and explode across the room. When describing his boulder problems, his excitement becomes uncontrollable. His eyes shine, his fists clench, he grits his teeth and growls, pantomiming the cruxes. He searches for words to match his enthusiasm and ends up inventing new ones midsentence.

". . . you slap to this gleck sloper, *whaaaaaatisch!*, then get into this total fungo position, like this? Then *Buhdoooogis!*, up to the most mackadocious pinch in the world. Then *dooooogis!* to this horrendous crimp, and *doogis, doogis, doogis* to the top. It's so *doooooope!* You're gonna love it!"

A true New Yorker, Ivan's not given to understatement. In New York you have to shout to be heard, dress to be seen, and rush to arrive or you find yourself ignored, invisible, lost. My own tendency is to meet hyperbole with cautious skepticism. "Hmmm," I said to Ivan, casually nodding my head. "That sounds pretty good . . ." But as he continued his impassioned descriptions, I noticed a tingle of excitement spreading through me. Various shoulder and forearm muscles were contracting involuntarily, and I accidentally chalked up while standing there listening.

A few weeks later, a route-setting delay at a competition in New Paltz provided a spur-of-the-moment opportunity for Ivan to show off his creations to the East Coast posse. The day was gray and cold, but we optimistically piled into his Saab and jetted up to the Trapps, stereo bumping Notorious

B.I.G. beats so deep that we were bouncing on the seats, occasionally banging our heads on the ceiling. Though we were due back at the comp for finals in two hours, we were pretty sure they wouldn't start without us. All of the finalists were in the car.

Ivan screeched around the corners, pumping his fists in the air and shouting at the top of his lungs over the music. His words alternated between Biggie's rap lyrics and tidbits of beta for his most recent masterpiece, the Illustrious Buddha.

We tumbled out the doors like shell-shocked clowns from a sensory-overload circus car and followed Ivan on a mad-dash tour down the Carriage Road, stopping at classic problems established as far back as the '60s by legends like John Gill, Lynn Hill, Patrick Edlinger, and Jerry Moffatt. Ivan tried to keep us moving, pausing just long enough to point out each problem, watch everybody fall a couple of times, then casually hike it with perfectly wired beta— he couldn't have been happier. Then he'd quickly throw his sneakers back on and hop around yelling, "C'mon, you gumbs! Stop flailing and send this thing so we can get to the biz!" As we moved in fits and starts toward the Illustrious Buddha, we gathered quite a crew, and a sense of competition hung in the air like chalk dust in a gym. Even as one climber splattered on the crash pad, the next contender was eagerly hopping over him to grab the start holds.

By the time we reached our destination, a drizzle had begun and dark was setting in. Our skin was wearing down, we were shivering, and the finals were supposed to begin any minute now, back in town. My first thought on seeing the boulder was, "Oh look, here's a nice big roof we can hide from the rain under. I wonder where the Buddha is?" My next thought was, "Why is Ivan putting chalk on that flat spot? Why is he pretending to lift himself up there . . . ? Wait a minute . . ."

Ivan stood under the huge, prow-shaped, horizontal roof. His arms were spread wide above his head, bear hugging the prow on opposing flat spots. He squeezed his arms together, straining so hard that his pectorals bulged to their full C-cup potential. He arched his back and piked his feet off the ground and into two small toehook notches. His body clung horizontally, with one flat spot and one toehook on either ride of the prow. As all his friends and rivals stood around, too wide-eyed to spot, Ivan performed the bizarre and complicated sequence he had choreographed to climb the Illustrious Buddha.

I was blown away. I had looked at this boulder and seen only shelter—the thought of climbing it had not even occurred to me. This is not a boulder that begs to be climbed. It's not particularly high, nor does it have anything that looks much like a hold—just a series of acute and obtuse angles. But by imaginatively fitting the parts of his body on and around these angles, Ivan had created a subtle, dramatic, and beautiful boulder problem.

When he finished, the rush began. Oblivious to the drizzle, the cold, the impending dusk, and any thoughts of conserving strength for the finals, we threw ourselves at these fascinating moves while Ivan fed us the kind of genuinely encouraging beta that can only be supplied by someone who has just resoundingly sent the problem in everyone's face.

After numerous inglorious backflops, I finally managed to hoist myself up onto the four non-holds that start the problem. One move was about all I managed that session, but what an incredible move! My body had never done that before, and my mind could still hardly believe that it worked.

By the time we tore ourselves away, my brain was spinning fast, repeating that opening movement again and again, then leaping forward to future visits, dreaming up as-yet unimagined moves on unseen boulders. Ivan promised enormous untouched potential in the area, and my skepticism was waning.

II. From the minds of sick individuals come sick boulder problems. *To them, every new and difficult movement is a great one, and the hardest way is almost always the best. Gather a collection of such twisted people, and their intensity is magnified by one another through lenses of competition and camaraderie, then focused to a pinpoint on a single objective: one boulder, one move, one hold. The result is explosive.*

Ivan, along with Marc Russo and a handful of other New Paltz and New Jersey climbers, had been establishing problems for about a year before our eye-opening session on the Illustrious Buddha. With that visit, a new group energy was ignited, and the pace of development exploded.

The converts included climbers from all over the Northeast. After gathering in The Bakery for coffee-chugging and rabble-rousing, we'd head out en masse, usually to the cliffs and talus fields of Peter's Kill, a section of Minnewaska State Park recently opened to climbing thanks to the efforts of the Access Fund. The boulders there, virtually untouched in the spring, held well over a hundred problems by fall.

On my first visit to Peter's Kill, I put up several obvious new problems. The movements were difficult and unique, and their realization sweet . . . for about ten minutes. Then on to the next! The thrill of newness kept me coming back all year, making the pilgrimage from Connecticut at least twice a week.

My mileage was outdone, however, by the driving exploits of Obe Carrion, whose six-hour round-trip journeys from Pennsylvania were fueled by a maniacal drive to send absolutely everything. The beginning of the season was back-to-school time for Obe. His obvious strength and talent were raw, fresh out of the gym, and he bashed himself against every hard move in the area trying to keep up with Ivan. By late spring he had learned the subtleties of Gunks rock, and the rest of the season became an ever-escalating frenzy of hard new development as Obe and Ivan strove to outdo each other, move by move.

Between problems, the two of them would race around the forest bugging out. Singing rap lyrics, attacking each other with Mortal Kombat moves—the most popular move, the Snake Style, was a two-fingered jab to the throat—and spotting intriguing boulders through the trees. They'd push each other out of the way to get the first crack at a newly spied line, then battle furiously for the first ascent. The beta was refined with each burn, a higher hold was reached, and the competitive fever rose.

"C'mon, Hector," Ivan would say. "You better send this thing right now, cuz I'm about to walk it."

"Who you callin' Hector, yo?" growled Obe, chalking his hands and mustering his psych. "Y'ain't walkin' nothin'. I'mma show you how we do it Puerto Rican style." He'd put his head down and mutter to himself, "C'mon Obe, c'mon. C'mon Obe, c'mon!" then step to the rock.

Obe climbs to a self-produced soundtrack—a human beatbox of rhythmic exhalations that coordinate his timing and remind him to keep breathing. "F-T-PAAAA!" he shouts after sticking a deadpoint, "F-T-PAAAA!" While holding a deep, static lock-off and delicately reaching to a far-off hold, his breath escapes in a loud, slow hiss: "SSSSSSSSSSSSSSSSSS . . ." And on reaching the hold, an explosion of relief: ". . . SSSSS-PAAAAAAA!"

He holds nothing back, and you can see the struggle in the contorted grimace of his face. He fully expects his body to be capable of anything his mind asks it to do, and those are often tall orders. "I feel I should be able to on-sight every boulder problem I try," he's told me. "But sometimes my brain can see me doin' it before I have the physical capabilities of doin' it, and that's when I get upset."

Obe puts so much pressure on himself that outside observers sometimes wonder where the fun is. "Why don't you try to relax?" I've heard people ask him.

"Relax?" he replied. "Man, I can't be relaxin'. This is what I do. This is everything to me. If I was relaxin' I'd have no boulder problems done. I'd be lyin' on a beach somewhere, and I'd be relaxed."

With Ivan screaming "C'moooon! I got you! Go! I got you!" Obe would dig as deep as he could. When successful, his joy was unrestrained. He'd jump around on top of the boulder shouting nonsense victory cries in Spanish and laugh contagiously the rest of the day. Other times he'd run out of steam and crumple to the ground with a moan of exasperation. "Dude, you were there!" Ivan would cry triumphantly, hopping over Obe's fallen body for his chance to snag the first ascent. "Why'd you fall, you gumb?"

"I don't know, yo. I don't know. Just punch me in the back of my head," said Obe. "Then send that freakin' thing," he'd add. "It's easy anyway."

III. Group synergy can transform the humblest of boulders into climbing monuments. *After a project's been sent, the rock seems bigger, somehow more important. The chalked holds, like footprints across a deserted beach, provide a sense of human scale. The pain and frustration involved in mastering the movement is forgotten, leaving a completed and enduring thing of beauty: a boulder problem.*

It's two years later and things have changed in the Gunks— it's an area now. I recently ran into two strong, well-traveled boulderers out at Peter's Kill. They had driven from Colorado, planning to tour the eastern half of the United States for a couple of months. But after bouldering at the Gunks, their first stop, they scrapped their plans to go anywhere else.

I could hardly believe it. I'd had a particularly mortifying climbing day, and I felt fed up with the tip-shredding, tendon-tweaking, sharp, little, hard-to-hold, goddamn crimpers. I'd had enough of the finicky conditions, torturous sit-down starts, and head-and-coccyx-smashing talus landings. I just wanted to get the hell out of there and go to a "real" area.

"I think this place is just as good as Hueco or Fontainebleau," one of the guys told me.

When I found Ivan at another boulder and related the encounter, he was equally confused. "Are they smoking crack?" he asked. "Are they bugging?" Even Ivan, after three years of screaming the glories of Gunks bouldering to the world, had never dared such a sacrilegious comparison.

We dismissed the matter laughingly and went on bouldering, but I kept noticing Ivan slipping into a mood unusual for him: calm reflection. As for myself, I stared at the all-too-familiar boulders, trying to see them through fresh, outside eyes. Despite my frustrating day, I still had a deep respect for the bouldering here. But I also suspected that much of the reason I liked the area was because it was "ours."

"They're really not going anywhere else?" Ivan asked me that evening as we stood around the parking lot slowly stuffing our crashpads into the car. "I can't believe those guys."

"Yeah," I replied, "crazy." I was looking down at my feet, which were scuffling around idly in the parking lot gravel. A long silence passed, and it occurred to me that long silences almost never pass in the company of Ivan. After some time I looked up and added, "But it still makes me kinda happy."

Ivan broke out into a triumphant little foot-stomping dance, threw his head straight back, and screamed up into the sky "WOOOOOOOORRRRRD!!!!!!!"

IV. Creativity and enthusiasm ensure great bouldering—the rock is a secondary resource. *People with minds demented enough to spend days torturing their bodies in the pursuit of horrendously difficult and utterly meaningless goals will find opportunities to do so wherever they may be.*

Besides being my main climbing partner, Ivan is also my boss at Chelsea Piers, a deluxe Manhattan sports club with a huge climbing wall. He hired me during the frenzy of bouldering development in the Gunks and coordinated our schedules so he'd have a partner every week.

At work, when we weren't training endurance or keeping the members from falling to their death, Ivan and I would relive the past week's bouldering exploits with the rapt attention of our fellow employees.

Preston Lear was always particularly attentive. Preston had moved to New York City from Salt Lake, resolved to the unavoidable fact that he'd be sacrificing his climbing habit for the rigors of the big-city academic life. He'd been surprised to hear of the bouldering scene up in the Gunks, just an hour and a half from Manhattan, but with a busy school schedule, a wife and dog, and no car, he only managed to taste it for himself a couple of times.

Ivan and I would act out all the beta for the newest crop of problems, argue the names and grades, and compare sore muscles. Preston, who hadn't touched real rock for months, would spend hours soaking up vicarious bouldering thrills. He was desperately in need of a fix, and besides, anything was better than loading the dishwasher with dirty holds or spraying down the rental shoes with Lysol.

During one of these bullshitting sessions, Preston arrived at work practically skipping with excitement. "Dudes," he said, "the Gunks sound great and all, but today I've seen my future, and it's a boulder in Central Park."

"You mean Rat Rock?" yawned Ivan. "That shit is played."

"No, no, no!" Preston exclaimed. "This boulder is a little bit off the beaten path. It's way uptown, actually. Actually," he stammered, "it's in Harlem."

A small bunch of New York City climbers had known about the spot for a while and had done a few moderate problems. But Preston had become obsessed with the idea of a traverse. Over the following months, we heard about the bewildered looks he got during his uptown subway rides with a crashpad on his back, though he assured us that, while the neighborhood was run down and dominated by housing projects, he felt totally safe bouldering there. Particularly when accompanied by Roman, his 120-pound rottweiler.

Preston was making gradual progress on the traverse, and it was shaping up to be hard. We noticed him training more. Seems he got in the habit of making dawn pilgrimages to his beloved boulder to squeeze in a couple of burns on the project before his 9:00 a.m. class. "You guys should come check it out," he'd say, but somehow the invitation seemed halfhearted.

That changed as soon as he sent the traverse. No longer protective of his cherished project, he went into full hype mode, bombarding us with beta and cooing, "It's soooooo gooooooood!" Ivan and I were reluctant to make the journey all the way to Harlem for one little traverse. We were both on rest days preparing for "important" projects in the Gunks, and besides, how hard could this thing really be? Did he really want to drag us all the way up there just to watch us rudely flash his pride and joy?

"Dudes," he said, with a knowing twinkle in his eye, "I'd love to see someone flash it." He shook his head, preparing to deliver the clincher, "But I really don't think it's possible."

So off we went, with Ivan driving and Preston waxing poetic about the Harlem boulder. "It's actually really high quality. But more than the climbing," continued Preston, who's studying for his masters in social work at NYU, "this whole thing's been a pretty intense cultural experience."

I'd long been picturing the super-solid rock and nicely textured slopers Preston was always going on about, but now he started filling in the rest of the picture. "One thing you guys should know," he warned us. "In this part of the park there aren't any public bathrooms . . . and, uh . . . I guess this rock provides the most privacy around."

"Oh no," I moaned.

"It's not exactly a pristine wilderness," Preston went on. "In fact, when I first started coming here the whole area was covered with broken glass, and there were crack vials, syringes, and condoms all over the place."

"Fantastic! Why are you taking us here?" I said.

"What the dilly, yo?" said Ivan.

"It's not that bad now, though," continued Preston. "I met this ambulance driver here one day, and he gave me a box of quadruple-thick, needle-proof rubber gloves so I could pick up all the trash. I filled a whole garbage bag!"

"Damn," said Ivan.

"Jesus Christ," I said.

"Yeah, there's usually some sketchy characters around, too," admitted Preston. "But there's always cops nearby. Last time this cop car pulled up right next to the boulder and the guy leaned out the window and yelled, 'Hey you!' I thought he was gonna hassle me about climbing, but listen to this— he goes, 'Watch yourself around here. We pulled a corpse out of the bushes behind that rock yesterday!'"

By now we were pulling up to a parking spot next to the edge of the park, across from a burnt-out building. It was too late to turn around. "Preston," I said, "this better be good."

Preston zoomed ahead on his skateboard while Ivan and I lagged behind, scoping out a bunch of outcrops along the way. When we arrived at the boulder, Preston made us do every warm-up problem before he showed us his creation, *Family Values.*

As soon as I started fondling the traverse's holds, I was fascinated. There were all sorts of complicated slopers, the kind you can stand and study for minutes at a time. Tunnel vision eliminated all perception beyond the surface of the boulder, and I was transported straight out of Harlem. I had come up here expecting a silly, half-assed session on some obscure piece of rock, but as I prepared to try the traverse I felt a calm, intense focus sweeping over me. This was the real deal. I flashed the problem with perfect beta from Preston, and it felt as significant as anything I'd ever done.

After that, we upped the ante with a desperate four-move addition to the beginning of the traverse. Ivan was also in serious bouldering mode, and after devising a crazy heel hook sequence, he was ready to send.

We gave him a good spot and fed him continuous encouragement. But as Ivan began the problem, a gang of punks stopped on the path behind us for some after-school fun. "Yo, white boys!" they screamed at us in prepubescent voices. "What the fuck you doin'?"

There were two of us, shirts off, kneeling on a little fuzzy mattress and reaching out toward the back of a third shirt-less guy who was hanging onto that rock where people go to shoot up and take shits.

"You faggots or something?"

Ivan, who was in the middle of the crux, tried to maintain his composure. All he had to do was hit that next good edge, and he'd be in for sure. "Yo! Faggot! I'mma put a cap in yo' ass!"

Ivan slowly unwound onto the sloper he had just crossed to, coiling like a spring beneath the good edge and looking right at it. He froze for a second, and shook with body tension, unbreathing and turning red.

"Do it!" we shouted. "C'mooooon!"

"Homo!" screamed the kids.

And Ivan sprung, his body exploding off the wall, his hand shooting up to snag the edge, his feet flying out in a huge arc. A tremendous cry of "Flacco!" drowned out all other noises.

"Flacco?" I asked him later. "Why'd you say Flacco? That means 'skinny' in Spanish."

"I dunno," he said. "I was just focused on doing the move. That's what came out."

Watching Ivan's performance on the first ascent of *Sweat of the Rapist*, Preston once again saw a vision of his future. Preston is a patient, determined climber who picks an objective and stays with it to the end. When he had done *Sweat*, he moved onto another project, and several months later added *Privileged*, a four-move line up the center bulge on ridiculous nothings. By now, he guesses he's made more trips to this obscure little boulder in the middle of Hell than to any other climbing area. He's hauled out bags of hazardous waste, and hauled in bags of wood chips. And he's dragged dozens of climbers there, who, like myself, arrived horrified and left inspired.

Every boulder problem begins in the mind. . . .

THE SCHRECKHORN (1871)
Leslie Stephen

Most people, I imagine, have occasionally sympathised with
the presumptuous gentleman who wished that he had been
consulted at the creation of the world. It is painfully easy
for a dweller in Bedfordshire or the Great Sahara to suggest material improvements in the form of the earth's surface. There are, however, two or three districts in which
the architecture of nature displays so marvellous a fertility
of design, and such exquisite powers of grouping the various elements of beauty, that the builders of the Parthenon
or of the noblest Gothic cathedrals could scarcely have
altered them for the better. Faults may of course be found
with many of the details; a landscape gardener would throw
in a lake here, there he would substitute a precipice for a
gentle incline, and elsewhere he would crown a mountain
by a more aspiring summit or base it on a more imposing
mass. Still I will venture to maintain that there are districts
where it is captious to find fault; and foremost amongst them
I should place the three best-known glacier systems of the
Alps. Each of them is distinguished by characteristic beauties. The mighty dome of Mont Blanc, soaring high above
the ranges of aiguilles, much as St. Paul's rises above the
spires of the City churches, is perhaps the noblest of single
mountain masses. The intricate labyrinths of ice and snow

The Swiss Alps

that spread westwards from Monte Rosa, amongst the high peaks of the Pennine range, are worthy of their central monument, the unrivalled obelisk of the Matterhorn. But neither Chamounix nor Zermatt, in my opinion, is equal in grandeur and originality of design to the Bernese Oberland. No earthly object that I have seen approaches in grandeur to the stupendous mountain wall whose battlements overhang in midair the villages of Lauterbrunnen and Grindelwald; the lower hills that rise beneath it, like the long Atlantic rollers beaten back from the granite cliffs on our western coast, are a most effective contrast to its stern magnificence; in the whole Alps there is no ice-stream to be compared to the noble Aletsch glacier, sweeping in one majestic curve from the crest of the ridge down to the forests of the Rhone valley; no mountains, not even the aiguilles of Mont Blanc, or the Matterhorn itself, can show a more graceful outline than the Eiger—that monster, as we may fancy, in the act of bounding from the earth; and the Wetterhorn, with its huge basement of cliffs contrasted with the snowy cone that soars so lightly into the air above, seems to me to be a very masterpiece in a singularly difficult style; but indeed every one of the seven familiar summits, whose very names stand alone in the Alps for poetical significance—the Maiden, the Monk, the Ogre, the Storm Pike, the Terror Pike, and the Dark Aar Pike—would each repay the most careful study of the youthful designer. Four of these, the Jungfrau, Mönch, Eiger, and Wetterhorn, stand like watchhouses on the edge of the cliffs. The Jungfrau was the second of the higher peaks to be climbed; its summit was reached in 1828, more than forty years after Saussure's first ascent of Mont Blanc. The others, together with the Finsteraarhorn and Aletschhorn, had fallen before the zeal of Swiss, German, and English travellers; but in 1861 the Schreckhorn, the most savage and forbidding of all in its aspect, still frowned defiance upon all comers.

The Schreckhörner form a ridge of rocky peaks, forking into two ridges about its centre, the ground plan of which may thus be compared to the letter Y. The foot of this Y represents the northern extremity and is formed by the massive Mettenberg, whose broad faces of cliff divide the two glaciers at Grindelwald. Halfway along the stem rises the point called the Little Schreckhorn. The two chief summits rise close together at the point where the Y forks. The thicker of the two branches represents the black line of cliffs running down to the Abschwung; the thinner represents the range of the Strahlhörner, crossed by the Strahleck pass close to its origin. Mr. Anderson, in the first series of *Peaks and Passes*, describes an attempt to ascend the Schreckhorn, made by him under most unfavourable circumstances; one of his guides, amongst other misfortunes, being knocked down by a falling stone, whilst the whole party were nearly swept away by an avalanche. His courage, however, did not meet with the reward it fully deserved, as bad weather made it impossible for him to attempt more than the Little Schreckhorn, the summit of which he succeeded in reaching. A more successful attack had been made by M. M. Desor and Escher von der Linth in 1842. Starting from the Strahleck, they had climbed, with considerable difficulty, to a ridge leading apparently to the summit of the Schreckhorn. After following this for some distance, they were brought to a standstill by a sudden depression some ten or twelve feet in depth, which was succeeded by a very sharp arête of snow. Whilst they were hesitating what to do, one of the guides, in spite of a warning shriek from his companions, and without waiting for a rope, suddenly sprang down so as to alight astride of the ridge. They followed him more cautiously, and, animated to the task by a full view of the summit, forced their way slowly along a very narrow and dangerous arête. They reached the top at last triumphantly, and, looking round at the view, discovered, to their no small disgust, that to the north of them was another summit. They had indeed proved, by a trigonometrical observation, that that on which they stood was the highest; but in spite of trigonometry, the northern peak persisted in looking down on them. As it was cut off from them by a long and impracticable arête some three hundred yards (in my opinion, more) in length, they could do nothing but return and obtain another trigonometrical observation. This time the northern peak came out twenty-seven metres (about eighty-eight feet) the higher. It was, apparently, the harder piece of work. Even big Ulrich Lauener (who, I must admit, is rather given to croaking) once said to me, it was like the Matterhorn, big above and little below, and he would have nothing to do with it. In 1861, however, the prestige of the mountains was rapidly declining. Many a noble peak, which a few years before had written itself inaccessible in all guide-books, hotel registers, and poetical descriptions of the Alps, had fallen an easy victim to the skill and courage of Swiss guides and the ambition of their employers. In spite, there-fore, of the supposed difficulties, I was strongly attracted by the charms of this last unconquered stronghold of the Oberland. Was there not some infinitesimal niche in history to be occupied by its successful assailant? The Schreckhorn will probably outlast even the British Constitution and the Thirty-nine Articles: So long as it lasts, and so long as Murray and Baedeker describe its wonders for the benefit of successive generations of tourists, its first conqueror may be carried down to posterity by clinging to its skirts. If ambition whispered some such nonsense to my ear, and if I did not reply that we are all destined to immortal fame so long as parish registers and the second column of the *Times* survives, I hope to be not too severely blamed. I was old enough to know better, it is true; but this happened some years ago, and since then I have had time to repent of many things.

Accordingly, on the night of August 13, 1861, I found myself the occupant of a small hole under a big rock near the northern foot of the Strahleck. Owing to bad diplomacy, I was encumbered with three guides—Peter and Christian Michel and Christian Kaufmann—all of them good men, but one, if not two, too many. As the gray morning light gradually stole into our burrow, I woke up with a sense of lively impatience—not diminished, perhaps, by the fact that one side of me seemed to be permanently impressed with every knob in a singularly cross-grained bit of rock, and the other with every bone in Kaufmann's body. Swallowing a bit of bread, I declared myself ready. An early start is of course always desirable before a hard day's work, but it rises to be almost agreeable after a hard night's rest. This did not seem to be old Peter Michel's opinion. He is the very model of a short, thick, broad mountaineer, with the constitution of a piece of seasoned oak; a placid, not to say stolid, temper; and an illimitable appetite. He sat opposite me for some half-hour, calmly munching bread and cheese, and meat and butter, at four in the morning, on a frozen bit of turf, under a big stone, as if it were the most reasonable thing a man could do under the circumstances, and as though such things as the Schreckhorn and impatient tourists had no existence. A fortnight before, as I was told, he had calmly sat out all night, halfway up the Eiger, with a stream of freezing water trickling over him, accompanied by an unlucky German, whose feet received frostbites on that occasion from which they were still in danger, while old Michel had not a chilblain.

And here let me make one remark, to save repetition in the following pages. I utterly repudiate the doctrine that alpine travellers are or ought to be the heroes of alpine adventures. The true way at least to describe all my alpine ascents is that Michel or Anderegg or Lauener succeeded in performing a feat requiring skill, strength, and courage, the difficulty of which was much increased by the difficulty of taking with him his knapsack and his employer. If any passages in the succeeding pages convey the impression that I claim any credit except that of following better men than myself with decent ability, I disavow them in advance and do penance for them in my heart. Other travellers have been more independent: I speak for myself alone. Meanwhile I will only delay my narrative to denounce one other heresy—that, namely, which asserts that guides are a nuisance. Amongst the greatest of alpine pleasures is that of learning to appreciate the capacities and cultivate the goodwill of a singularly intelligent and worthy class of men. I wish that all men of the same class, in England and elsewhere, were as independent, well informed, and trustworthy as Swiss mountaineers! And now, having discharged my conscience, I turn to my story.

At last, about half-past four, we got deliberately under way. Our first two or three hours' work was easy enough. The two summits of the Schreckhorn form, as it were, the horns of a vast crescent of precipice which runs round a secondary glacier, on the eastern bank of the Grindelwald glacier. This glacier is skirted on the south by the ordinary Strahleck route. The cliffs above it are for the most part bare of snow and scored by deep trenches or gullies, the paths of avalanches, and of the still more terrible showers of stones which, in the later part of the day, may be seen every five minutes discharged down the flank of the mountain. I was very sanguine that we should reach the arête connecting the two peaks. I felt doubtful, however, whether we could pass along it to the summit, as it might be interrupted by some of those gaps which so nearly stopped Desor's party. Old

Michel indeed had declared, on a reconnoitering expedition I had made with him the day before, that he believed, "steif und fest," that we could get up. But as we climbed the glacier my faith in Michel and Co. began to sink, not from any failing in their skill as guides but from the enormous appetites which they still chose to exhibit. Every driblet of water seemed to be inseparably connected in their minds with a drop of brandy, and every flat stone suggested an open-air picnic. Perhaps my impatience rather exaggerated their delinquencies in this direction; but it was not till past seven, when we had deposited the heavy part of our baggage and, to my delight, most of the provisions on a ledge near the foot of the rocks, that they fairly woke up and settled to their task. From that time I had no more complaints to make. We soon got hard and steadily at work, climbing the rocks which form the southern bank of one of the deeply carved gullies of which I have spoken. It seemed clear to me that the summit of the Schreckhorn, which was invisible to us at present, was on the other side of this ravine, its northern bank being in fact formed by a huge buttress running straight down from the peak. This buttress was cut into steps by cliffs so steep as to be perfectly impracticable; in fact, I believe that in one place it absolutely overhung. It was therefore necessary to keep to the other side, but I felt an unpleasant suspicion that the head of the ravine might correspond with an impracticable gap in the arête.

Meanwhile we had simply a steady piece of rock climbing. Christian Michel, a first-rate cragsman, led the way. Kaufmann followed and, as we clung to the crannies and ledges of the rock, relieved his mind by sundry sarcasms as to the length of arm and leg which enabled me to reach points of support without putting my limbs out of joint—an advantage, to say the truth, which he could well afford to give away. The rocks were steep and slippery, and occasionally covered with a coat of ice. We were frequently flattened out against the rocks, like beasts of ill-repute nailed to a barn, with fingers and toes inserted into four different cracks, which tested the elasticity of our frames to the uttermost. Still our progress though slow was steady, and would have been agreeable if only our minds could have been at ease with regard to that detestable ravine. We could not obtain a glimpse of the final ridge, and we might be hopelessly stopped at the last step. Meanwhile, as we looked round, we could see the glacier basins gradually sinking and the sharp pyramid of the Finsteraarhorn shooting upward above them. Gradually, too, the distant ranges of Alps climbed higher and higher up the southern horizon. From Mont Blanc to Monte Rosa, and away to the distant Bernina, ridge beyond ridge rose into the sky, with many a well-remembered old friend amongst them. In two or three hours' work we had risen high enough to look over the ridge connecting the two peaks, down the long reaches of the Aar glaciers. A few minutes afterwards we caught sight of a row of black dots creeping over the snows of the Strahleck. With a telescope I could just distinguish a friend whom I had met the day before at Grindelwald. A loud shout from us brought back a faint reply or echo. We were already high above the pass. Still, however, that last arête remained pertinaciously invisible. A few more steps, if "steps" is a word applicable to progression by hands as well as feet, placed us at last on the great ridge of the mountain, looking down upon the Lauteraar Sattel. But the ridge rose between us and the peak into a kind of knob, which allowed only a few yards of it to be visible. The present route, as I believe, leads to the ridge at the point farther from the summit of the mountain. We were, however, near the point where a late melancholy accident will, it is to be hoped, impress upon future travellers the necessity for a scrupulous adherence to all recognised precautions. The scene was in itself significant enough for men of weak nerves. Taking a drop of brandy all round, we turned to the assault, feeling that a few yards more would decide the question. On our right hand the long slopes of snow ran down toward the Lauteraar Sattel, as straight as if the long furrows on their surface had been drawn by a ruler. They were in a most ticklish state. The snow seemed to be piled up like loose sand, at the highest angle of rest, and almost without cohesion. The fall of a pebble or a handful of snow was sufficient to detach a layer, which slid smoothly down the long slopes with a low ominous hiss. Clinging, however, to the rocks which formed the crest of the ridge, we dug our feet as far as possible into the older snow beneath and crept cautiously along. As soon as there was room on the arête, we took to the rocks again and began with breathless expectation climbing the knob of which I have spoken. The top of the mountain could not remain much longer concealed. A few yards more, and it came full in view. The next step revealed to me not only the mountaintop but a lovely and almost level ridge which connected it with our standing point. We had won the victory and, with a sense of intense satisfaction, attacked the short ridge which still divided us from our object. It is melancholy to observe the shockingly bad state of repair of the higher peaks, and the present was no exception to the rule. Loose stones rattled down the mountainsides at every step, and the ridge itself might be compared to the ingenious contrivance which surmounts the walls of gaols with a nicely balanced pile of loose bricks—supposing the interstices in this case to be filled with snow. We crept, however, cautiously along the parapet, glancing down the mighty cliffs beneath us, and then, at two steps more, we proudly stepped (at 11:40) onto the little level platform which forms the "allerhöchste Spitze" of the Schreckhorn.

I need hardly remark that our first proceeding was to give a hearty cheer, which was faintly returned by the friends who were still watching us from the Strahleck. My next was to sit down, in the warm and perfectly calm summer air, to enjoy a pipe and the beauties of nature, whilst my guides erected a cairn of stones round a large black flag which we had brought up to confute cavillers. Mountaintops are always more or less impressive in one way—namely, from the giddy cliffs which surround them. But the more distant prospects from them may be divided into two classes: those from the Wetterhorn, Jungfrau, or Monte Rosa, and other similar mountains, which include on one side the lowland countries, forming a contrast to the rough mountain ranges; and those from mountains standing, not on the edge, but in the very centre of the regions of frost and desolation. The Schreckhorn (like the Finsteraarhorn) is a grand example of this latter kind. Four great glaciers seem to radiate from its base. The great Oberland peaks—the Finsteraarhorn, Jungfrau, Mönch, Eiger, and Wetterhorn—stand round in a grim circle, showing their bare faces of precipitous rock across the dreary wastes of snow. At your feet are the "urns of the silent snow," from which the glaciers of Grindelwald draw the supplies that enable them to descend far into the regions of cultivated land, trickling down like great damp icicles, of insignificant mass compared with these mighty reservoirs. You are in the centre of a whole district of desolation, suggesting a landscape from Greenland, or an imaginary picture of England in the glacial epoch, with shores yet unvisited by the irrepressible Gulf Stream. The charm of such views—little as they are generally appreciated by professed admirers of the picturesque—is to my taste unique, though not easily explained to unbelievers. They have a certain soothing influence, like slow and stately music, or one of the strange opium dreams described by De Quincey. If his journey in the mail-coach could have led him through an alpine pass instead of the quiet Cumberland hills, he would have seen visions still more poetical than that of the minster in the "dream fugue." Unable as I am to bend his bow, I can only say that there is something almost unearthly in the sight of enormous spaces of hill and plain, apparently unsubstantial as a mountain mist, glimmering away to the indistinct horizon, and as it were spellbound by an absolute and eternal silence. The sentiment may be very different when a storm is raging and nothing is visible but the black ribs of the mountains glaring at you through rents in the clouds; but on that perfect day on the top of the Schreckhorn, where not a wreath of vapour was to be seen under the whole vast canopy of the sky, a delicious lazy sense of calm repose was the appropriate frame of mind. One felt as if some immortal being, with no particular duties upon his hands, might be calmly sitting upon those desolate rocks and watching the little shadowy wrinkles of the plain, that were really mountain ranges, rise and fall through slow geological epochs. I had no companion to disturb my reverie or introduce discordant associations. An hour passed like a few minutes, but there were still difficulties to be encountered, which would have made any longer delay unadvisable. I therefore added a few touches to our cairn and then turned to the descent.

It is a general opinion, with which I do not agree, that the descent of slippery or difficult rock is harder than the ascent. My guides, however, seemed to be fully convinced of it; or perhaps they merely wished to prove, in opposition to my skeptical remarks, that there was some use in having three guides. Accordingly, whilst Christian Michel led the way, old Peter and Kaufmann persisted in planting themselves steadily in some safe nook, and then hauling at the rope round my waist. By a violent exertion and throwing all my weight onto the rope, I gradually got myself paid slowly out and descended to the next ledge, feeling as if I should be impressed with a permanent groove to which ropes might be fixed in future. The process was laborious, not to say painful, and I was sincerely glad when the idea dawned upon the good fellows that I might be trusted to use my limbs more freely. *Surtout point de zèle* is occasionally a good motto for guides as well as ministers.

I have suffered worse things on awkward places from the irregular enthusiasm of my companions. Never shall I forget a venerable guide at Kippel, whose glory depended on the fact that his name was mentioned in The Book, viz. *Murray's Guide*. Having done nothing all day to maintain his reputation, he seized a favourable opportunity as we were descending a narrow arête of snow, and suddenly clutching my coattails, on pretence of steadying me, brought me with a jerk into a sitting position. My urgent remonstrances only produced bursts of patois, mixed with complacent chucklings, and I was forced to resign myself to the fate of being pulled backwards, all in a heap, about every third step along the arête. The process gave the old gentleman such evident pleasure that I ceased to complain.

On the present occasion my guides were far more reasonable, and I would never complain of a little extra caution. We were soon going along steadily enough, though the slippery nature of the rocks, and the precautions necessary to avoid dislodging loose stones, made our progress rather slow. At length, however, with that instinct which good guides always show, and in which amateurs are most deficient, we came exactly to the point where we had left our knapsacks. We were now standing close to the ravine I have mentioned. Suddenly I heard a low hiss close by me, and looking round saw a stream of snow shooting rapidly down the gully like a long white serpent. It was the most insidious enemy of the mountaineer—an avalanche; not such as thunders down the cliffs of the Jungfrau, ready to break every bone in your body, but the calm malicious avalanche which would take you quietly off your legs, wrap you up in a sheet of snow, and bury you in a crevasse for a few hundred years, without making any noise about it. The stream was so narrow and well defined that I could easily have stepped across it; still it was rather annoying, inasmuch as immediately below us was a broad fringe of snow ending in a bergschrund, the whole being in what travellers used to represent as the normal condition of mountain snow—such that a stone, or even a hasty expression, rashly dropped, would probably start an avalanche. Christian Michel showed himself equal to the occasion. Choosing a deep trench in the snow—the channel of one of these avalanches—from which the upper layer of snow was cut away, he turned his face to the slope and dug his toes deeply into the firmer snow beneath. We followed, trying in every way to secure our hold of the treacherous footing. Every little bit of snow that we kicked aside started a young avalanche on its own account. By degrees, however, we reached the edge of a very broad and repulsive-looking bergschrund. Unfixing the rope we gave Kaufmann one end and sent him carefully across a long and very shaky-looking bridge of snow. He got safely across, and we cautiously followed him, one by one. As the last man reached the other side, we felt that our dangers were over. It was now about five o'clock.

We agreed to descend by the Strahleck. Great delay was caused by our discovering that even on the nearly level surface there was a sheet of ice formed, which required many a weary step to be cut. It was long before we could reach the rocks and take off the rope for a race home down the slopes of snow.

As we reached our burrow we were gratified with one of the most glorious sights of the mountains. A huge cloud, which looked at least as lofty as the Eiger, rested with one extremity of its base on the Eiger and the other on the Mettenberg, shooting its white pinnacles high up into the sunshine above. Through the mighty arched gateway thus formed, we could see far over the successive ranges of inferior mountains, standing like flat shades one behind another. The lower slopes of the Mettenberg glowed with a deep blood-red, and the more distant hills passed through every shade of blue, purple, and rose-coloured hues into the faint blue of the distant Jura, with one gleam of green sky beyond. In the midst of the hills the Lake of Thun lay, shining like gold. A few peals of thunder echoed along the glacier valley, telling us of the storm that was raging over Grindelwald.

It was half-past seven when we reached our lair. We consequently had to pass another night there—a necessity which would have been easily avoided by a little more activity in the morning.

It is a laudable custom to conclude narratives of mountain ascents by a compliment to the guides who have displayed their skill and courage. Here, however, I shall venture to deviate from the ordinary practice by recording an anecdote, which may be instructive and which well deserves to be remembered by visitors to Grindelwald. The guides of the Oberland have an occasional weakness, which Englishmen cannot condemn with a very clear conscience, for the consumption of strong drink; and it happened that the younger Michel was one day descending the well-known path which leads from the chalet above the so-called Eismeer to Grindelwald in an unduly convivial frame of mind. Just above the point where mules are generally left, the path runs close to the edge of an overhanging cliff, the rocks below having been scooped out by the glacier in old days, when the glacier was several hundred feet above its present level. The dangerous place is guarded by a wooden rail, which unluckily terminates before the cliff is quite passed. Michel, guiding himself as it may be supposed by the rail, very naturally stepped over the cliff when the guidance was prematurely withdrawn. I cannot state the vertical height through which he must have fallen onto a bed of hard uncompromising rock. I think, however, that I am within the mark in saying that it cannot have been much less than a hundred feet. It would have been a less dangerous experiment to step from the roof of the tallest house in London to the kerbstone below. Michel lay at the bottom all night, and next morning shook himself, got up, and walked home sober, and with no broken bones. I submit two morals for the choice of my readers, being quite unable, after much reflection, to decide which is the more appropriate. The first is: Don't get drunk when you have to walk along the edge of an alpine cliff; the second is: Get drunk if you are likely to fall over an alpine cliff. In any case, see that Michel is in his normal state of sobriety when you take him for a guide, and carry the brandy flask in your own pocket.

TAWOCHE: A RETROSPECTIVELY PLEASURABLE ASCENT (1996)

Mick Fowler

Our base camp at just over five thousand meters was the highest I'd ever had, and not being a quick acclimatizer I was still nursing a throbbing headache after the first week. Potentially I might have been looking even less healthy than our liaison officer. He was a Tourism Ministry official based in Kathmandu who had never been to the mountains of the Khumbu region before. Whilst he shivered in the cold and looked distinctly unhappy, he could at least count the very substantial wad of money he was accumulating. I had no such compensating thoughts, and lay uncomfortably in the tent whilst Pat Littlejohn, British guide, rock climber extraordinaire, and, on this trip, my climbing companion, displayed a distressing amount of energy, even to the extent of wandering up to the foot of the unclimbed northeast buttress of Tawoche (6,542 meters) to check out the line a French team had tried in 1990. He returned exuberant, to find me still in my sleeping bag whining about my head. Apparently he had spotted some overhanging grooves, which he felt should offer what he described as "wonderful climbing."

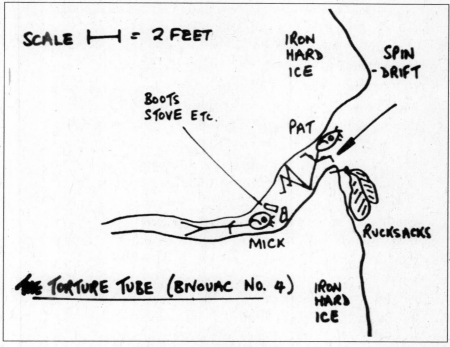

Tawoche: A Retrospectively Pleasurable Ascent (1996)
Illustration by Mick Fowler, originally published in American Alpine
Journal, *38 (1996): 52*

I managed to delay things by two days, but inevitably the
time came when we approached the climb together—feeling
very small beneath the huge expanse of verticality rearing up
above us. The aim of the day was to climb up an overhanging
rock band at the foot of a prominent ramp line leading up to
the crest of the buttress.

"Looks good, doesn't it?" Pat's enthusiasm was clearly
not diminished by our imposing surroundings. I wasn't sure.

The line he was pointing at looked to overhang disturbingly. I was glad I'd left my rock boots at home.

"Important to keep the weight down," I explained to an incredulous Pat. It all looked horribly difficult as I sat comfortably watching the proceedings from my well-protected belay.

The heroic rock master inched his way up through the overhangs and then—even more impressively—back down again.

"1 don't think that's right." He was soon off again on another line. I watched intrigued as he tried several times to make progress using a tiny, dubious-looking undercut. A good nut protected the move and looked to be an ideal handhold. Pat, though, was clearly reluctant to stoop to my own "pull-on-it-if-it's easier" Himalayan ethics so early in the climb. And so we continued for two hundred feet or so, Pat laybacking, bridging, and whooping with joy whilst I struggled along behind with double boots and a large sack.

By late morning we had reached a sheltered belay just to one side of the toe of the ramp. Above us the heat of the day was now bringing down too many large icicles interspersed with rocks to justify continuing. In any event the main aim of the day was complete and the way to the ramp was open. Keen to ensure that we could regain this point as quickly as possible, we abseiled down, leaving our ropes in place, and headed off back down to base camp.

Two days later we were back. Our big effort was under way.

"Are you sure you've got your slings the right length?"

The owner of the voice wafting down from above was clearly aware that the Fowler body was having a bit of trouble. His concern was fully justified. This rope-climbing business is supposed to be fast and energy-efficient, and yet here I was after fifteen minutes of maximum effort hanging upside down, completely knackered and only a few inches above the ground.

The problems seemed numerous, the main one being my sack, which had the distressing effect of pulling me backward in such a way that I was unable to push the Jumar clamps up the rope. Improvisations flowed thick and fast, but the only thing that seemed to make any difference was attaching my rucksack chest straps into the top Jumar. This partially strangled me and seriously restricted the Jumar movement but at least enabled some limited progress to be made. In retrospect I'd have been better off seconding the pitches again. Pat seemed to find all this particularly funny, if rather incomprehensible. (I suppose guides aren't allowed to revel in incompetence in the same way as us amateurish types.)

Meanwhile, I hung from the rope in full gasping-fish mode, vowing to take jumaring lessons at some stage in life. Above us the ramp looked challenging. The French had been up here in 1990, and soon a despicable bolt gave a clue as to their abseil line. Pausing to spit on such an unethical eyesore, we scrambled up awkward mixed ground, heading out to the objectively safe but technically difficult-looking right-hand edge of the horribly huge and intimidating ramp. Pat led a distressingly difficult pitch and belayed in an awkward-looking position. He pointed gleefully at his belay—a huge wedged flake sitting precariously in a loose seventy-five-foot groove.

"You can either climb over this and kill us both if it comes off or lead out onto that featureless slab."

Out on the slab, I was soon in a world where slivers of rock peeled off readily under scraping crampons. I gibbered badly. The French obviously hadn't come this way.

"What's it like?"

"Retrospectively pleasurable, Patrick."

This was to be our pet phrase for the route. It's often true, of course, if you think about it. After several more retrospectively pleasurable pitches, Pat stopped at a horizontal knife-edge crest.

"Bedtime, Michael."

I looked around hopefully. We had arrived at the prominent shoulder on the northeast buttress, the first real landmark, and reached well within our projected time scale. My hopeful look was soon turning into an acceptance that it would be one of those special nights astride an ice crest or perched with one buttock on a six-inch-wide ice ledge. Pat, though, likes his comfort and started the ice crest with a worrying degree of enthusiasm. The man clearly wasn't as tired as he should have been. Not feeling so energetic, I positioned myself such that I could contribute by ineffectually flicking my ice ax pick at the iron-hard ice. The end result was a campsite perched right on the crest. It lacked amenities and was only big enough for about two-thirds of the floor area of the tent, but I had to admit that it was an awful lot more comfortable than my suggestion of a "perch-on-your-bum" bivouac.

Two pitches farther up and we found our final piece of equipment from the French 1990 attempt. The report in the *American Alpine Journal* said that they ground to a halt in the face of "soft snow and technical difficulties." Looking up, the technical difficulties were all too apparent. I just hoped that the white stuff snaking down the corner lines was ice and not the feared soft snow. We had chosen the pre-monsoon season hoping that the powder snow problems experienced by the French would not be so acute. On that front we seemed to have made the right decision. The downside, though, was the weather pattern. It snowed every afternoon, and I mean *every* afternoon. By the end of day four on the face, I was getting a bit sick of this. The climbing was difficult, time-consuming work up steep, ice-plastered grooves which tended to act as chutes for huge quantities of the stuff. Frequently heavy waves of it would catch me unawares and snow would force its way deep down the front of my jacket.

During our fourth day a prominent ramp line had taken us round to the right side of the buttress when the afternoon's onslaught hit us with even greater ferocity than usual. A bivouac where we were was out of the question, but up to the left was a glimmer of hope—a snow patch and, though I couldn't be sure, what looked like the entrance to a small cave. Pat had been stationary for a long time whilst I prattled about losing sight under the waves of snow. Not being a fan of inactivity, he jumped at my suggestion that he get some exercise and warm up by climbing a difficult-looking corner that led to the bivouac. Dusk found us both hanging from an ice screw just outside a very constricted-looking ice hole with a substantial lip of iron-hard ice overhanging the entrance.

"Doesn't look very nice, does it?"

Pat sounded disheartened. He doesn't like discomfort. As I was (in Pat's eyes) the Master of Uncomfortable Bivouacs, I felt obliged to sound a bit more enthusiastic.

"Be fine once we've dozed off."

Keen to demonstrate this—and even more keen to surround myself in nice, warm, cozy down—I thrust my sleeping bag into the entrance and squeezed in. It was even worse than it had looked. At the entrance the diameter was probably two feet or so, but the feature was more of a wind-formed ice tube than a conventional cave. It sloped downward at about forty-five degrees for six feet before leveling off. Unfortunately, though, by the time it leveled out it had narrowed to about twelve inches across by eighteen inches high. I lay on my side, at the bottom. Even my weedy shoulders and hips were too broad to turn over. I tried hard to control a rising sense of claustrophobia and keep smiling whilst Pat's swearing up above suggested that the entrance area was uncomfortable if less claustrophobic. Every now and then various objects would be dropped down on me: a thermos, Pat's boots, the stove . . .

I was staring intently at the stove wondering how to position myself to make a brew when there was a distinct and unexpected change for the worse. The wind, which up to now had been in our favor, had clearly changed; suddenly it was as if a fireman had directed his hose straight into my bedroom. Spindrift piled up with alarming speed, immediately burying everything Pat had dropped down to me. My initial concern was keeping the snow out of my sleeping bag. I lifted the entrance out of the main flow, but the volume was such that within seconds my priorities had changed and I was more concerned that I would be trapped inside the tube by a wall of spindrift. Abandoning every other thought, I fought to extricate myself from this cold and constricted hellhole and fight my way back to the surface. This proved challenging in the smooth forty-five-degree section. My struggles and screams prompted comments of the "I thought you liked this kind of thing" category but at least had the desired end result. The night, though, was but young as I dived head first in an effort to retrieve boots and stove whilst Pat grappled with the complexities of extracting the tent and arranging the fabric in such a way that we could both be at least partially protected . . .

And so began what was undoubtedly the most uncomfortable night of my life. We were both supposed to have the tent over our heads, but the angle of the tube was such that my head was level with Pat's feet. I spent the night trying to prevent myself from sliding down into oblivion by holding onto the fabric around the door whilst Pat cursed and swore about the pressure on his head and shoulders. Fortunately for me it wasn't until much later that we realized that my efforts and Pat's problems were connected. We never did manage to get into our sleeping bags again: the awkwardness of the situation, fear of melting spindrift freezing the down, and a conviction that we should make it anyway tempted us to stay as we were.

After twelve hours of minus twenty-five degrees C or so, a blast of sunlight is decidedly welcome. Unfortunately, though, our hole (or the "Torture Tube" as we now familiarly referred to it) was mean to the last and necessitated ten feet of climbing before we could soak up the sun. Surprisingly enough, our first pitch of the next day was only ten feet long.

Bright sunlight and calm weather have a remarkably positive effect on the body. By the end of the first full-length pitch, the rigors of the Torture Tube were receding and our minds were fully engrossed in the climbing difficulties. We were just to the right of the crest of the buttress now and, as this was the north side, we feared that the permanently subzero temperatures would allow a buildup of bottomless powder snow. Our binoculars had revealed very steep white streaks hereabouts, and we were prepared for a precarious wallow. How wrong can one be?

Distressingly steep streaks of hard ice soared up for hundreds of feet. In places they were truly vertical. Pat was belayed below what was clearly to be the first really steep pure ice pitch.

"How many ice screws have we got?"

"Er . . . three."

I sheepishly recalled throwing out the extras that Pat had packed, insisting that three would be sufficient. Somehow one ice screw at each stance and one for a runner didn't seem very satisfactory now that we were here. Very careful climbing ensued for a few pitches until the inevitable afternoon spindrift onslaught started.

A hole up to our left beckoned uncomfortably: I was wary of holes after the Torture Tube. This one, though, looked different. Initial impressions were quite good: It was an ice hole which pierced the crest of the sixty-five-degree buttress but was perhaps three feet high, four feet across, and five feet long. It had a flat floor, and one of the finest views in the world. To the east Makalu, Everest, and Ama Dablam with the east face of Tawoche dropping away below; to the west Cho Oyu, Cholatse, and below us the unclimbed north face of Tawoche. Unfortunately, it was clearly created by the wind, which duly started to gust through our "campsite" as we struggled to establish ourselves in our half-erected tent. Inside, the fabric flapped incessantly and hoar frost rained down.

"Why do we do this, Patrick?"

"You like it. Michael. Makes holidays more memorable."

I lay back and contemplated. It was true, of course, that if everything went according to plan, life would be pretty boring. Inside my sleeping bag life was warm and cozy and dry—pretty good, really. I was glad that we'd suffered the sleeping bag–less masochism of the Torture Tube and kept our sleeping bags dry.

We were somewhere near the top of the buttress now, but it was difficult to say how close. Above us was that very special sort of uncertain ground: very steep and very white. It was Pat's turn to lead the first pitch of the day whilst I belayed uncomfortably in the tunnel, which had become even colder and windier without the blocking and protective qualities of the tent. I concluded from Pat's progress that the first pitch was (very) hard ice where, judging by his comments, more than three ice screws would have been distinctly useful. By the time I was engrossed in the second pitch, the daily dose of bad weather was again closing in fast.

"Watch out," Pat had said. "Belay's not very good."

These words kept repeating uncomfortably in my head as I struggled away in my own little white, windswept world. Somewhere above me was the top of the buttress. I should be able to do it in one pitch if only I control myself on the ice screw placements.

Somehow, precarious ice climbing seems so much more difficult when you have to keep looking down. But judging how far I had come and weighing the distance up against the fear factor was the only way to limit my protection to the means available. It felt a long pitch: Soon I couldn't see Pat any longer and concentrated on my last screw and the ground ahead. The end came all rather suddenly. There was hardly any easing of the angle, just a sudden realization that I was about to swing my ax into thin air over a narrow snow crest.

The other side of the crest was easy-angled. It felt strange after five and a half days of steep, technical ground. Walking has never been my strong point, but here I felt even less attuned than usual to the joys of stumbling over bottomless powder. Pat seemed not to be so badly afflicted by loss of balance and general lethargy. Strong chaps, these guides—far too much energy.

A solitary glimpse of the summit was all we were to get that night before staggering off along the not-very-obvious ridge leading in its general direction. Somewhere in the limitless white, an area that looked to be flat enough to pitch the tent materialized, and we collapsed in a horizontal position, lost in our cozy sleeping bags and lulled asleep by the purring stove.

It was a memorably pleasant experience to wake up and find we were much closer to the summit than expected. Perhaps half an hour above us was the top of Tawoche. Being terribly English, we shook hands formally on the top. I think we were even emotional enough to manage a (very) small French-style hug.

"Look at all these things to do." Pat was bouncing around enthusiastically. Meanwhile I contemplated whether I could summon the energy to rotate my body sufficiently to manage a summit panorama from a sitting position. I could . . . And now back in Britain I too am able to enthuse about the numerous unclimbed possibilities the world has to offer. I have to agree with Pat's on-the-spot assessment.

"There's still a lot to be done."

And he is even older than I. There's hope for a few more years yet.

EXPLORING THE YOSEMITE POINT COULOIR (1939)

David Brower

"Why don't some of you young experts try the long gully leading to Yosemite Point?"

Coming from Charles Michael, who for decades had been exploring Yosemite's out-of-the-way places, this was more than a question. It was a challenge, experts or no. And so it was that noon of June 8, 1938, found Morgan Harris, Torcom Bedayan, and me munching sandwiches, drinking occasionally from a tiny rill, and relaxing on white, avalanche-polished granite, halfway up the deep couloir marking the joint-plane between Yosemite Point and Castle Cliffs. Below us was the scene of our morning's travail—the level Valley floor we had left early that morning (quarter to nine is early for rock climbers), the old and obscured Indian Canyon Trail we had followed to the base of Castle Cliffs, the shoulder stand, the airy traverse, and the bushwhack that had marked our crossing under the cliffs to the couloir. Immediately under us was the pitch that we imagined had stopped all predecessors some fourteen feet above the Valley. Indeed, it might well have stopped us had not Morgan obligingly taken the rope up ahead, exhibiting friction climbing that I would freely have explained as impossible had I not seen it. Here he had used our first piton, and belaying from below I had quietly wondered how much good it would have done in an emergency. The pitch was a polished slab, nearly holdless, and even after Torcom had followed Morgan's route I was still certain that it was too steep for tennis shoes—mine, at any rate. I had fudged a little by finding a more exposed variation to the right, with good old-fashioned holds that did not strain the imagination.

But that was all below, now. Above us the steep walls of the couloir, massive granite towering eighteen hundred feet to the north rim, clearly defined our route as the floor of the couloir—a floor with an average angle of forty-five degrees for its full length of forty-five hundred feet. Ahead of us a hundred feet was the first chockstone. Above that we recalled having seen a second from the Valley. What lay beyond?

Well, for one thing, there were two trails beyond, leading right to the top of the climb. One crosses from the top of Yosemite Falls. The other is the old Indian Canyon Trail, so long abandoned that trees nearly forty years old grow in the middle of it. But as dyed-in-the-wool rock climbers we weren't interested in trails and preferred to see Yosemite the hard way. We had interpreted Charles Michael's question to mean that this was one of the hardest ways, and with a reaction peculiar to rock climbers had set out to investigate. Besides, we felt an added zest in exploring new routes rather than spending our time reviewing old ones. Specific lessons in retracing steps could better be learned on the rocks of the Bay region.

Bestirring ourselves with difficulty after lunch, we walked a short distance over rounded talus, mixed with a sprinkling of scree, until the vertical walls of the couloir converged and at some time in the distant past had said "no thoroughfare"

The Yosemite

David Brower in 1993

to one of the largest talus blocks of them all. From a distance I had seen an easy way to climb out around the left side, using a shoulder stand. But close examination revealed that even a three-man stand couldn't pass a twenty-five-foot overhang. There were no piton cracks, no holds. In the cavern beneath the chockstone there was a bit of indirect light, but none of us felt small enough to find how it filtered through. The wall on the right seemed worse.

Back in Berkeley, when we first learned the lore of piton-craft, vast horizons had opened up before us. Nothing could be impossible. Pitons had conquered the Cathedral Spires.

Why could not the sheer faces of Half Dome and El Capitan or the slender spire of the Lost Arrow be as summarily dealt with? Of course the horizon soon closed in. Frustrated attempts on the "firefall route" up Glacier Point, the west face of the Sentinel, and even on little Pulpit Rock had clearly demonstrated that it would take more than a little hardware to make boulevards in lichen-land. Here we were, again, with a knapsack full of pitons, stymied.

No. There was a possibility—a break in that right wall some thirty feet back down the gully, connecting with a ledge that paralleled the floor. At least there was a chance; so standing on Torcom's shoulder to surmount a slight overhang, I began resolutely to pound in pitons, unscrupulously relying upon direct aid to progress another ten feet up an open chimney, simply because there was no other way to get up. Then there were no more piton cracks. Threading the rope through the existing pitons and carabiners in several sequences and thus affording a variety of cross-tensions, I leaned out from the face at all angles. But in the eight remaining feet of rounded granite I could perceive no route that was the least bit interesting. So I retired to the base and Morgan took the relief shift. While belaying, he had pointed out a way, a traverse to the left, which I had been loath to undertake. It involved getting farther away from the top piton and higher above the gully floor, so I explained that there weren't enough holds to use. Morgan, quite unsympathetically, proceeded to use this route, and standing on the last hold, partially supported by the pull of the rope through the top piton, he drove in another. But here he ran into difficulty. Being only five-foot-eleven, the stretch to the next hold was beyond his reach. So back I went, six-foot-one and all, with the correct combination freshly in mind. Precisely how or why, I don't recall, but I was soon on the ledge. I do remember, however, a bit of delicate maneuvering, where an extra pound of pressure in the wrong direction would have meant starting all over. The ledge was treacherously covered with scree, narrow, sloping out and down, and devoid of piton cracks for twenty feet, so that success left me feeling no more secure. Driving a star drill (a rock climber's knapsack has everything) in to the hilt in scree for what security it might offer, I crawled up these twenty feet, placed a piton, and Torcom followed as second man. Proceeding up the ledge to a point level with the top of the chockstone, I was trying to discover a route across the intervening blank wall when the most alarming of rock climbers' cries, "Rock!" rent the air. I was not particularly alarmed by the cry, since it was mine; but it was disconcerting to watch a five-pound missile bound toward us in long, hissing ricochets from the walls, with no good chance to dodge. After it had struck the face six feet in front of me and had glanced on to skim over Morg, he and I assured Torc that this was nothing at all—that the summer before on Glacier Point many rocks passed us at so high a velocity we couldn't see them, and had only a crescendo and diminuendo as a clue to their proximity.

Of course no one who passes an afternoon in a long chute that has been carved by rock and snow avalanches should be surprised to hear a falling rock now and then. There is a very definite objective danger. But we had weighed our chances carefully. Yosemite granite is particularly massive and sound, and I knew, from having lived more than two years in the Valley, that rockfalls on the north side were rare even in winter. We accordingly felt even now that the chances of surviving objective hazards were better than those of avoiding automobile accidents, and I continued to lead. Piton No. 9, placed as high as I could reach above the ledge, permitted a rope traverse across the blank face, and with a final jump I was on the spacious roof of the chockstone.

To pass away the time while waiting for me to decide where to go, Torcom had been salvaging pitons from the route, for we still did not know what was ahead and were particularly anxious not to run short of safety equipment. Consequently, by the time Torcom reached the top of the chockstone it was no longer possible to protect Morgan with an upper belay along our route, nor was there anyone left to give him the shoulder stand necessary to start the pitch. So we dropped two ropes, one to belay him as he climbed the other hand over hand. With the belayer supplying some additional pull, the scheme worked admirably, and Morgan was up the twenty-five-foot overhang in just about ten seconds.

So engaged with the first chockstone had we been that we failed to notice the shadows on the Valley floor, which were becoming ominously long. Not being anxious to spend the night searching for the route with flashlights, we began to climb with all speed, calling upon every technique that would serve to put our climbing team out on top before dark. Morgan took the lead up under the second chockstone, and showered us with dirt as he cleaned off a route for a traverse over its edge. Changing the lead whenever it saved time, giving the second and third men an occasional tug with the rope if they lagged, standing in pools of water, or slithering on granite wet by the rill we had so prematurely blessed at noon, we hurried on. A third chockstone was conquered with the aid of a four-sided chimney behind it; long slabs of forty-five-degree granite were ascended with varying forms of cross-pressure. We could now see by the serration of the tops of the walls that we were near the end. But still all was not well. Although at times tempting, the walls were still quite inaccessible, and ahead we could hear the persistent drip of a tiny waterfall formed by our little rill. In the deep shadow it was not possible to know just what we were up against, but we knew the ascent of a waterfall, however small, is likely to be complicated.

With wet tennis shoes, Morgan traversed from the security of a three-sided chimney from which Torcom belayed him, around a polished nose into an open, two-sided affair, the sides of which were polished, rounded, at angles of approximately 120 degrees to each other and forty-five to fifty degrees from vertical. Somehow he found sufficient cross-pressure to supplement the few minute holds and advanced steadily to the source of the drip, a full twenty feet above us. Piton No. 10 went into place on the left wall, and he traversed diagonally upward to his right. There was thrilling suspense for a moment as he paused at the brink of the "waterfall," cautioning us to be ready for a fall, then very deliberately pulled himself up, settling into belay position. From our comfortable spot below, Torcom and I had spoken all the encouragement we could, which is the least the supporting party can do for its leader; but it wasn't until we climbed the pitch with an upper belay that we realized how much more encouragement Morgan deserved. Coming up as third man I couldn't discover how he led the pitch, and still don't know. While I prefer to think it was because we were hurried and I was carrying the pack, I nevertheless had to use that forbidden handhold—the rope.

Eleven hours of roped climbing were over. The gully opened out into a ravine, then into a rocky basin. Soon we were in the open, out among the Jeffrey pines and manzanita, with soft, friendly soil to walk upon. Below to the west Yosemite Creek, in full flood, rushed down its hanging valley, obscured in the shadows of dusk. Across it was the trail we wanted, and although we knew that it was inaccessible because the bridge was out, we were not troubled. For with the remnants of the Indian Canyon Trail, the intervening thickets of chaparral, and the rockslides of "big-jump" talus, we knew we could somehow reconstruct a way down to the Valley—covering in a day the newest and oldest of north-wall routes.

We struck off for the head of the canyon, with the freshness of High Sierra springtime in the cool air, the music of falling water interrupted by an occasionally spirited yodel, our shadows, cast by the rising moon, on the pine needles and snowbanks underfoot.

A TALE OF TWO EPICS (2006)

Paul Ross

Part I: The West Face

In 1955 I read a book about the first ascent of the West Face of the Aiguille du Dru by Guido Magnone. I was only eighteen, but I was so impressed with this mountain that I thought if I could ever do this route, my life's climbing ambitions would be fulfilled. Then, in 1957, I was off to the French Alps for two weeks, my first alpine season.

The trip out was an epic. A friend and I started off on a motorbike with a sidecar and ended up breaking down only fifty miles into France. We took the train the rest of the way to Chamonix. My only mountaineering experience up to that point was on the small crags and hills of the Lake District.

In Chamonix, I couldn't take my eyes off the massive-looking mountains, yet not for one moment did I feel intimidated. Rather, I was impatient to get up there. A climbing friend from the Lakes and I quickly did two climbs. Although not big routes, the Pointe Albert (ED) and the Aiguille de Moine (TD) gave us no trouble and we easily beat the guidebook times. They also gave us an idea of French alpine climbing grades. Now what?

Someone said a bloke named Joe ("Morty") Smith, a young member of the famed Rock and Ice club, was looking for a partner to have a go at the West Face of the Dru. At that time, the only British climbers that had done this route were two other Rock and Ice members, Joe Brown and Don Whillans.

I had never met Morty, but I had heard of him—actually nothing to do with his climbing ability but about his tea-making exploits when camping with his older Rock and Ice mates. His reputation came from his cooking skills and hygiene habits. The tea episode I had heard about amounted to his club members giving him the task of making cups of tea for them, which they figured Morty, in spite of his reputation, could not screw up. He succeeded with the brewing but had problems trying to get condensed milk out of two small holes he had punched into the top of the can. He solved the problem by sucking mouthfuls of condensed milk out of one of the holes and spitting it into each cup.

I met Morty at the Chamonix swimming pool. After a few grunts from his gravel Manchester and my Cumbrian/Geordie accent, we were committed and planned to take on what was then considered one of the most technical routes in the western Alps. The other major climb—the Bonatti Pillar, on the same face of the Dru—had been climbed by then, but little was known about it.

I was well equipped. I had bought a pair of pointy-toed Lachenal alpine boots, but I had worn the front part of the Vibram sole down to the screws on my first two climbs, so I opted to use my old, floppy Gimmer hiking boots. The right boot had a two-inch ax cut down one side as a result of my forestry work, and it had stretched to need three pairs of socks. But it had good rubber.

My knee breeches were tailored by my mother from my old grammar (high) school suit pants. The rest of my alpine clothing consisted of an Army string vest, a smart shirt, a wool sweater, a new $12 feather (mostly stems) duvet jacket, a camouflaged cotton Army wind parka, and the famed Pack-a-Mac, a very thin, ladies' plastic rain coat with a hood. The Mac folded up to about the size of half an apple. The British bivy sack of the day consisted of a giant sheet of see-through plastic from the hardware store, sealed with Scotch tape into a two-man, plastic, pull-over-the-head device. It had a couple of vent holes so one would not suffocate, which I believe did happen on at least one occasion. The homemade bivy bag had many drawbacks, but the biggest was condensation. Too long a stay and one would get as damp as sitting outside in the rain—but it was warm.

Hard hats had yet to be invented. Morty had a flat cap; my head was bare. Morty's clothing was not much better, but he did sport a brand-new pair of highly polished alpine boots that made his clothing look even shabbier.

I asked Morty what we should take as far as pitons and wooden wedges, as there were major aid pitches on the West Face route. Four Polish climbers had just done the first Polish ascent; I think it had taken them four days. We found them at the campsite in pretty beat-up condition. They had had an epic ascent. Some of them had gotten frostbite—it made me think for a moment that it might be a tough climb for us young lads! Regardless, we asked them about pitons. They rattled off a list of at least thirty various pitons and numerous wooden wedges. Morty's theory was they had been slow because they took too much gear, and he declared that all we needed was three pitons and a wooden wedge that I had made from a broken ax shaft. I was not too happy about the decision, but as he was one alpine season ahead of me, I did not protest much. He also said we would be able to pick up more pitons as we went up the route. Anyway, I resolved to smuggle four more pitons.

We set off with fairly light packs. The choice of rations for two to three days consisted of a couple of tubes of condensed milk, some precooked bacon, powdered soup, tea, boiled sweets, and my few packs of cigarettes (they were still healthy in those days), and, of course, the greasy German sausage Morty carried in his trouser pocket. Every now and then he pulled it out, wiped off the fluff, and offered me a bite. I always declined. He would bite a chunk off, say it was great, and stuff it back in his pocket.

A few hours' walk from Montenvers across the Mer de Glace brought us to our bivy site below the twenty-five-hundred-foot face. All night, stones fell down the couloir we planned to climb. Magnone's book mentioned that (a lot), but Morty seemed unperturbed, so I figured it must be normal. Today, I would not consider going near the place.

We roped up below the couloir while dodging rocks that came at us with bulletlike speed. The thousand-foot couloir was a nightmare. Every ten minutes or so the rocks would come, the larger ones the size of footballs. There'd be a bang as they ricocheted off the walls and a whistling hum as they soared past us, our bodies pressed into the ice. I looked with envy on Morty's flat cap and pulled my parka hood over my head. I thought it might keep my scull together if I sustained a direct hit.

It was about this time that Morty started singing the first verse and chorus of the folk song "Midnight Special" in a raspy imitation of Louis Armstrong:

If you ever go to Houston boy, you better walk right,
you better not stagger and you better not fight,
for the sheriff will arrest you and will send you down.
Let the midnight special shine a light on me,
let the midnight special shine an ever-loving light on me . . .

I guess it had a calming effect on him.

With my bendy boots, I had problems trying to kick steps in the hard, frozen snow, but at last we crossed the wide stone chute where the couloir narrowed, and with great relief started up the shattered terraces that led to the center of the West Face. Finally, we were on solid rock. I quickly led the Fissure Vignes, finding little difficulty in what was supposed to be the crux-free pitch. We were moving very fast, and as Morty had prophesied, we collected pitons that had fallen from the frozen fingers of previous parties on the upper aid pitches.

Then we heard thunder. Oh shit. Lightning was dancing around the summits near the Grépon, and without doubt it was coming our way. A decision had to be made. Morty suggested we carry on until the storm hit, bivy, and wait it out. We would be hanging out on very steep technical rock. I did not like that idea. In the back of my mind was the question of retreat down that desperately dangerous couloir. We came to a compromise. We would abseil back to the terraces and wait to see if the storm was as bad as it looked.

Morty suggested we have some soup. He got out our gas stove and threw a handful of very old snow into our dixie pot. As the snow melted, I looked in the pot. There were dozens of tiny slugs, moving as fast as they could, as the water heated.

"Hey, Morty. What about these bloody things?"

Morty, quite unperturbed, said, "You won't notice them."

Then he poured in the powdered soup, stirring it with a hand unwashed (I think) since he left Manchester several weeks back. He also pulled out his pocket sausage and kindly offered a bite. I declined the sausage and drank the lesser of the two evils. Then the storm hit us. There was no question we had to descend the rest of the terraces and that bloody dreadful stone-raked couloir.

We reached the top of the couloir. Morty started abseiling across the stone chute and stopped in the middle, the rope a big ball of tangles. I thought, "Oh shit, this is it." Any minute now the stones are coming, and Morty—with the rope—is going, and I am staying a thousand feet up the Dru.

Morty was such a cool bugger, though. He just droned on, singing the "Midnight Special" and carefully sorting out the rope. At last he had enough to at least get out of the chute. He got a few feet from the side of the chute, and down came the rocks again. They whistled around him, some striking the rope. The smell of sulfur filled the air.

The heavens opened, lightning flashed in the couloir, torrential rain and hail and sleet filled the air. We couldn't tell the difference between the thunder and the crash of the rockfall. We were drenched and freezing. I thought, "This is really bloody serious," and wondered if we could survive the retreat. About every ten minutes or so the rocks, so absolutely terrifying, came.

I was envious of Morty with his flat cap as we crushed ourselves against the snow, my head covered with a cotton hood. My thin wool knee britches were starting to disintegrate, a lump of soggy sock was sticking out of the cut in the side of my boot; then the damn abseil rope got stuck, somewhere near the anchor.

Well, if we were going to hang around, the rocks or the lightning was going to get us. So without hesitation I "batmanned" the rope, freed it, and we continued. The rope did the same thing a bit farther down. Again, another dice with death, pulling hand over hand on the single stuck rope. The gods were with us. We reached the bottom, jumped the bergschrund, and ran like hell down the snow cone away from Skittle Alley.

More problems were at hand. It was almost dark, and we had to cross a heavily crevassed area (this area is now snow-free due to the warming trend in the Alps). Fortunately, we found our old footprints, which led us through a maze of threatening holes. It grew dark and was still storming like hell. Headtorches were unknown. In fact, neither of us owned a flashlight. What we had brought, at Morty's suggestion, was one candle, which under the circumstances was not really much help.

We reached solid ground. All we had to do was get down the moraine cliff and across the Mer de Glace to Montenvers in the dark. We sort of fell and rolled down the moraine cliff onto the Mer de Glace using Mother Nature as our flashlight—we just stood waiting for each lightning strike in order to get our bearings. It was a bit disconcerting as we had many iron carabiners attached to our bodies, and we felt a bit like mobile conductors. Massive claps of thunder and the lightning came simultaneously, and some of the strikes looked about fifty feet away and a foot thick. The whole glacier lit up each time, giving us a second to plot a course toward the ladders and steps that led up to the station at Montenvers. We got lost somewhere and ended up crawling on hands and knees over domes of wet, slippery ice above deep, yawning crevasses for what seemed hours. No crampons, of course. Me with a piton hammer in hand, and Morty, a bit more lucky, had somehow ended up with my North Wall hammer. My knee breeches by now had been reduced to ragged Robinson Crusoe–type shorts. We were both totally knackered when, after many, many lightning strikes, we found the steps to Montenvers and staggered up them to salvation. Just past the Montenvers rail station was our doss in the famed Chalet Austria, a tiny hut perhaps once used by shepherds.

Before the climb we had stayed in the hut. There had been some very friendly Austrians staying in the lower level. Banging on the door now, we pleaded for water, as we were desperately dehydrated. Shouts came back that we guessed were "fuck off" in Austrian, so we did without. Later, we learned a group of Brits from Wallasey had cleaned the upper floor of the hut and swept their rubbish though a hole in the floor onto the heads of the Austrians and laughed at their protests. My two-week alpine season was over. Well, I thought, nothing like learning the hard way. Now it was back to work and saving up for next year's alpine season.

Part II: Chamonix with Whillans

In the late spring of 1958, Don Whillans, whom I'd encountered and befriended a few years earlier, appeared back in Keswick after being on his first trip to the Himalayas, an expedition that had attempted to climb Masherbrum.

I should mention that young Whillans had many hang-ups with women, and his advances on my girlfriend (which were rejected) the previous year had possibly caused our first falling out. Then he made no mention to me that he was upset, and for a time we continued socializing, although I did realize he was being a bit more grumpy than usual. I then learnt he was telling friends of mine that he was going to fill me in, but he of course made no mention of this to me.

Anyway, one evening in that spring of 1958, I was sitting with friends in the Golden Lion, at that time the "climbers" pub, when in walked Whillans, looking fit and happy. Before he went to the bar, he walked straight up to me and, in a very jovial manner, asked if I wanted a pint. You could have knocked me down with a feather. Whillans going out of his way to buy someone a pint? More so, me, when several months earlier he had been saying (but not to me) that he was going to fill me in! Contrary to what was written in his book *Portrait of a Mountaineer*, he asked me if I wanted to go to the Alps and if I would go with him on his motorbike. I told him I had already arranged to go to the Alps and had a train ticket to Chamonix, but if he wanted I could meet him out there for the first part of my planned trip. He was enthusiastic and cheerful, and I thought, well, this must be the new Donald Desbrow Whillans. The Himalayan altitude must have done something to his brain.

The initial objective was to try and do the first British ascent of the Walker Spur on the Grand Jorasses. We met up in Chamonix and, as is quite often the case in the western Alps, the weather was bloody awful. Violent thunderstorms came in the afternoons; the Jorasses were snow covered. Our plan soon became seeing how many bars we could get to each and every night. The first sign of friction came after day one of camping together. That day, I had cooked the breakfast and dinner. The following morning, slightly hungover from our getting-into-shape drinking marathon, I waited for Whillans to prepare breakfast . . . and waited. Eventually I reminded him it was his turn. "Oh fuck" was his reply. Clearly, this was not part of Whillans's lifestyle. So I thought, "Fuck you, too." Being a cook and waiter was not part of mine either.

His compromise was to produce a very large bottle of vitamins (rare in those days) that he had acquired from his Himalayan expedition. These "magic" pills became his substitute for any call on him to do his share of camp cooking. I guess he thought I would weaken and eventually become his butler, but that never happened. It was pills during the day until we hit the bars and got a cheap meal of *pomme frites*, salad, and horse meat, followed by so much beer that the nightly hike back to camp through the woods became a staggering epic.

In those days, I had only two to three weeks off work per year. If, as now, the bad weather kept one from climbing, one just had to make the best of a bad job and have as good a holiday as possible. Running around bars and the discos of Chamonix trying to pick up girls was the only worthwhile recreation available. Of course, finding a French girl that would even think of dancing with a drunken Brit was much more difficult than any alpine climb. On about the fourth evening, with our welcome at some of the disco bars wearing out, our luck began to change.

At one of our watering holes, I returned to the bar and mentioned to Whillans that as I was selecting a record on the jukebox, two French girls sitting next to it seemed quite friendly, and one had said something to me in English.

Perhaps, as I was a whole two inches taller than Whillans's five-foot-three, he suggested I make an attempt to chat them up. Much to my surprise—due to previous attempts to chat up French ladies—they were very friendly and said they would like to go dancing. The older one, who was about twenty-four and spoke good English, told me she was a divorcée and at the same time said her nineteen-year-old sister, Jacqueline, was a virgin and had to stay that way. She was way, way ahead of me, and must have seen the look of shock on my face; I was just counting myself extremely lucky we had at last found someone of the opposite sex to dance with.

Whillans signaled to me he would take "care" of the older sister and, as I spoke a little French, I would escort the younger one who spoke no English. We all had a great evening rocking and rolling under the envious eyes of a large group of Oxford University climbers. I could see it would not be long before they would come and ask one of our ladies to dance. I quietly instructed Jacqueline in my best French that when an Englishman asked her to dance she should answer by saying "bugger off." The inevitable happened. A very polite chap came over and, with a slight bow, asked Jacqueline, "Voulez vous dancer avec moi?" With a beautiful smile, she replied, "Bugger off," and was puzzled at his abashed look and quick retreat. I realized it was a bit cruel on the guy. Anyway, it was the sort of humor that appealed to Whillans, who rolled around laughing.

Whillans, now full of confidence and beer, asked our new lady friends if they would like to come to our camp for coffee. I was somewhat surprised when they accepted, and I was pretty sure they would be coming for coffee and nothing else. But I don't think Whillans had the same assessment of the situation.

We reached the tent, and I had just started to make the coffee when Whillans suggested to the older sister that she get out of the chilly night air and join him in the tent. "Oh dear," I thought, "here goes nothing." She had just managed to get halfway though the tent entrance when Whillans made his move. It sounded like an all-out wrestling match with some quite impressive sound effects. It only lasted seconds, then the lady shot out of the tent followed by a volley of choice Anglo-Saxon profanities from Whillans. As a punishment, Whillans wanted to let them find their own way out of the woods in the pitch dark, and he was not pleased when I led them back to town.

Part III: The Bonatti Pillar

Our drinking and nighttime activities continued for a couple more days, then the weather seemed to improve. However, our Walker Spur ambition was out, due to heavy snow cover. Whillans suggested the Bonatti Pillar route on the Dru. It was too steep to hold the snow that had fallen over the last week, plus it had not yet had a British ascent. I jumped at this suggestion. Maybe this time my ambition to climb the Dru would materialize. We asked around but could not get a route description. We thought we'd be able to figure it out as we climbed.

This year I was better equipped. I had new alpine boots and a down jacket that was actually filled with down. Still no hard hats, but at least I now had a thick wool balaclava. My knee breeches were also better—an altered pair of my father's old deluxe cavalry twill trousers. My parka was the thin, ex-Army camouflaged jacket I had used the year before on the West Face, complemented by the usual cannot-do-without British ladies' plastic Pack-a-Mac.

The climbing equipment, of course, had not improved: two or three different sizes of soft iron pitons up to a half inch, plus slings and carabiners. Any type of nuts or camming devices were still unknown.

We set off across the Mer de Glace, then up to the base of the climb with packs bulging with food and long loafs of French bread strapped on top. We planned to bivy at the base and start up the dreaded couloirs at the crack of dawn. As we approached the face, we noticed four blokes watching our progress. They turned out to be Chris Bonington, Hamish MacInnes, and two Austrians, Walter Philip and Riccardo Blach. Whillans had met both MacInnes and Bonington, but I knew them by name only. Their plan was also the Bonatti, and they actually had a route description.

The next morning we set off up the couloir. Whillans, in his usual unselfish manner, had decided that he would have my North Wall hammer and left me with a five-inch piton for use as an ice tool. When I led through with my ice tool, I decided to avoid as much of the ice as possible, and, like the previous year when the stonefall was extremely heavy, I opted for a rock slab away from the center of the couloir. Unfortunately, this was a mistake, as rockfall had fractured and changed the slab. I was soon a hundred feet out with no protection. I prudently shouted to Whillans that I was staying put until he could climb above me and toprope me back onto the snow. In the mean-time, Philip, soloing, had gotten above Whillans and fallen on top of him. Luckily for us all, Whillans held on. Philip said sorry and continued his mad dash up the couloir.

It was not a good start, so different from Morty's and my uneventful ascent of this thousand-foot couloir the previous year—except for the frequent stonefall. Near the top of the couloir, Whillans put me in a very precarious position when he decided to take a shortcut down a rib of hard, frozen snow, leaving me to follow with my five-inch rock-piton ice tool. As he had no belay, a fall by me would have put us back at the bottom of the couloir. This was perhaps the most dangerous and frightening situation I experienced on the whole climb. It was with great relief we reached the foot of the pillar and somewhat solid granite. We swung leads up cracks and grooves. We arrived at a chimney/crack that according to the description was Grade VI and the most difficult free pitch on the route. We decided to haul the packs; to this point we had climbed with our packs on. This is where Whillans and I had our first confrontation. I led the pitch, which apart from getting around a loose flake, was no harder than 5.8.

From this point, Whillans's account and mine differ. I started to pull up the first pack, and midway up it swung into the corner. The North Wall hammer, strapped to the pack, jammed in one of the carabiners on the climbing rope (Whillans's description said I had clipped the hauling rope into the 'biner). Whillans then declared he would come up next and on the way free the pack. The first mistake he made was to try and climb it with his pack on. He was screaming "pull, pull" as his pack, in the constrictions in the groove, was giving him some problems. I pulled . . .

He eventually reached the jammed pack. I had already tied it off on a handy spike of rock. I had also tied him off with the intention of pulling the jammed pack up and out of his way. I shouted to him my plan, and he went berserk, screaming "how the fuck can you hold me and pull up the pack at the same time?"

Looking back, I think our week of training in the Chamonix bars and the altitude were having an effect on Whillans's brain and temper. So I let him continue in his own sweet way, me heaving as best I could until he rolled onto the narrow ledge well knackered. I waited until he had recovered, and explained that if he had listened he would have not had such a hard time of it.

That did it. He got to his feet, his nose an inch or two from mine, and said, "Who the fuck are you to tell me how to climb?" That also did it for me. I responded, "And who the fuck do you think you are?" Both of us now squared off, fists raised, on this tiny ledge. If I had biffed him it would have been a hundred-and-fifty-foot knockout, as he had yet to tie into the anchors.

I remember glancing down and seeing the anxious faces of MacInnes and Bonington as they watched these two very pissed-off dwarfs raging at each other. I think Whillans must have realized just how pissed off I really was, as he backed off, muttered a few more curses, and took off up the next pitch, which led to a big ledge that we would use for our first bivouac.

The four of us Brits now started to organize ourselves on the ledge; the Austrians were perched on another ledge about sixty feet above us. Very little time had passed before the sound of a falling rock made us all duck. It sounded rather like a thump on a bongo drum as it made a direct hit on the top of MacInnes's head (as I previously mentioned, hard hats were not in fashion in 1958). MacInnes slumped over, blood pouring from a nasty-looking scalp wound. Bonington's officers' training and Army first-aid kit came into use, and a field dressing stopped the bleeding, but MacInnes did not look too happy, to say the least. (We did not know it at the time, but he had apparently sustained a small skull fracture.) With this, all four of us became very paranoid about any further stonefall.

At the back of the ledge was a massive flake, leaning against the wall forming a small cave. MacInnes was laid inside this. Bonington and Whillans grabbed the positions closest to the wall, which would let them avoid any future missiles. My choice was either sit in front of them, a place where I'd likely be hit by rocks, or jam myself in a crack above MacInnes and hold myself in a standing position. I chose the latter, which meant I got very little sleep, as falling asleep would have dropped me on MacInnes's injured skull. I was more than pleased when that night was over. Throughout the night, rocks crashed down the couloir below us. The idea of retreat seemed much worse than the idea of trying to finish the climb.

Although the circumstances dictated it, I was happy when it was decided the Austrians would stay in the lead placing pitons (we had discovered a Swiss team that had made an ascent prior to ours had removed most of the expected fixed pitons), and I would be rid of grumpy Whillans, who now would take the groggy MacInnes in the middle team. Bonington and I would bring up the rear, me leading the free pitches and Bonington the aid.

The bivy ledge, due to our fear of more stonefall from the night before, was in complete disarray. Whillans decided we four Brits were carrying too much food and that we would climb faster if it were reduced by half. He asked if I would divide all the food and throw away the surplus. I placed the food into two plastic bags, and dropped one off the ledge as ordered. A few minutes later Whillans picked up the remaining bag of food, and by the time I noticed what he was up to, our remaining food was also off into space, and soon in the couloir a thousand feet below.

Fucking great, I thought. Besides the problems we already had, this bloke was turning the climb into a complete pain in the ass. I just wished I could walk away from the situation. I wasn't used to being on a climb with so little communication and companionship. The previous year on this same face with Morty Smith had been so different, even though we had to wait out a desperate storm and make an epic retreat. I had not had time to even speak to MacInnes before he was injured, but he seemed a nice, even-tempered sort of guy. Perhaps he was wondering what else could go wrong, and what his chances of making it off the mountain were.

As with MacInnes, I'd also had no real communication or socialization with Bonington. Bonington was a Sandhurst graduate (similar to West Point in the United States), and I think at that time he was an officer with the Royal Dragoon Guards. He now seemed to be behaving as such and acting as if Whillans was the commander-in-chief, backing up Whillans even though, I thought, he was fucking things up. As it happened, years later Bonington and I started climbing together both in the Lake District and the States and became firm friends.

In 1958 rescue from Grade VI climbs such as the Bonatti Pillar was unheard of. There was no such thing as a helicopter rescue from high-angled rock faces, and the rescue team consisted of Chamonix guides, who at that time were not highly trained technical climbers. So, in those days you were pretty much on your own if you attempted the most difficult alpine routes.

Ross and MacInnes on the Dru. Note MacInnes's bandaged head.
Paul Ross collection

The French girls I had met while bar-hopping with Whillans in Chamonix had been coming up to the Montenvers railway station and trying to find us through the telescopes. After our third day on the Dru, they still could not find us. The stationmaster noticed them each day, peering though the telescope, and asked them what they were looking for. They told him that a bunch of Brits were on the Bonatti and had been up there for three days. As it had stormed the previous night, he assured them we were more than likely dead. The sister told me later that Jacqueline had been crying when we had not turned up after two days.

Officer-in-charge Whillans was flustered at his fuck-up (throwing all our food down the Dru Couloir) but quickly announced that we did not really need it, as we would be off the climb by the following day. (In his book *Portrait of a Mountaineer*, Whillans makes no mention of why we ended up with no food.) I guess his optimistic prophecy was only off by three days. I could see by Bonington's expression that he, like I, was not too happy with the way things were going. We had a few scraps left (I don't remember the Austrians having anything at all). Bonington had somehow managed to save a few inch-size cubes of Army-issue oatmeal. I had some boiled candies that I shared, and someone had a couple of small packets of dried soup, but as there was no snow on this part of the climb, the soup was useless until our last bivy. This now meant two more days virtually without food or water. Even worse, both Whillans and I were running out of cigarettes!

The first half of the day went fairly well, Bonington doing the pitches that used some aid and I doing the free pitches while retrieving as many soft-iron pitons as possible. I had only one complaint: My piton hammer had somehow ended up with the Austrians. This was okay, but I had been left to do the de-pegging with a tool dubbed, by its proud owner MacInnes, "The Message." The Message was a slater's hammer with a steel shaft that MacInnes had chrome-plated—probably to improve its appearance. This monstrosity weighed a ton. Its head was way too large to fit in the back pocket of my pants, as was customary in those days (sophisticated gear like harnesses and holsters had yet to be invented). I tied its long leash to the bowline around my waist. It's no exaggeration to say that when you dropped The Message by its leash, it almost ripped you from the rock. It was exhausting to use with one hand, and it demolished the soft metal pitons if they put up any sort of resistance. I never did see this hammer come onto the market when MacInnes started manufacturing his other rock and ice climbing tools. It would have been, however, a great tool to discourage climbers from using pitons.

Quite early that next day, Bonington and I caught up with MacInnes and Whillans sitting on a ledge system. Above, Philip and Blach were hammering their way up thin cracks on a very steep, blank-looking face of pink granite. We sat and waited, passing up our total supply of pitons. They seemed to be going nowhere fast. After a few hours, it appeared to me this difficult aid climbing was just not in keeping with the rest of the route. I kept wondering what lay around a corner about twenty feet up and right of our ledge. I asked MacInnes, who was sitting beside me (Bonington and Whillans were on a ledge to our left), if anyone had been up there and had a look. The climbing looked easy, so I asked MacInnes to hold my rope so I could go and see what was around the corner.

I got about ten feet when Whillans noticed what I was doing. He threw another tantrum and started shouting "Where are you going? Come the fuck down." I started to argue, but MacInnes (both he and Bonington now seemed very intimidated by Whillans) said I had better come down. I was really pissed off.

After a while, Philip declared that the route he was on could not be the way, and they started to descend to our ledge. In Whillans's book *Portrait of a Mountaineer*, he says, "I set off to look for the correct route. I tried several possibilities." (In fact, there was only one possibility, and that was around the corner up to the right, which much earlier I had attempted to check out.) Whillans, of course, took full credit for finding the correct route. The route followed a chimney, then went up black overhanging rock filled with fixed pitons. By now it was almost dark, so he returned to the ledges, where we had just enough room to accommodate all six of us. We were now all suffering from lack of food, and no water had passed our lips for two days.

Part IV: Another Night, Another Day

Another long night followed. In his book, Whillans describes this bivy as such: "Hamish jammed himself into a chimney and prepared himself for another uncomfortable night . . . Paul, Walter, and Riccardo spread themselves out on the big ledge, leaving Chris and I sharing a smaller one lower down. The night was cold and dark mist swirled about us, etc."

My recollection of this delightful evening is a little different. MacInnes found a reasonably comfortable place around the corner in the bottom of a chimney. The "big" ledge that the Austrians and I were spread out on was sloping, and in order to fit, we had to sit with bent legs, using the friction of our boot soles to stay in place. Somehow the Austrian lads had managed to get behind me on the ledge, and throughout the night, when we'd all managed to doze off, their boot friction gave out, and they unwittingly pushed me forward, off the ledge (my tie-in had some slack). Each time I was left dangling in space. This happened numerous times, and after pulling myself back onto the ledge, we'd do a major reshuffle to get back into our positions. (Later on, I learned the pressure on my feet as I tried to stay on the ledge left me with mild frostbite in one of my big toes.)

I enjoyed some consolation listening to the grumbling coming from Bonington and Whillans on the small but flat ledge to our left. Unlike the Austrians and me, sitting out in the open enjoying the alpine air, they were inside the plastic bivy bag that Whillans and I had brought along. Although it gave some extra warmth, it also was providing both of them with something to complain about. Whillans was puffing away inside on his ciggies for much of the night, filling the bag with smoke. Bonington was coughing and quite angry. Whillans, meanwhile, was complaining about the dreadful smell.

Very early that day, Bonington had arrived on these ledges, and thinking we all would soon be much higher on the route, had dropped a pile in the middle of the ledge. This pile was now neatly stacked between them. Needless to say, it was a very long night.

The next morning the Austrians took off in the lead, Whillans and MacInnes followed, and Bonington and I brought up the rear, myself with the dreaded Message hammer trying to remove as many pitons as possible. No one had had water for two days, but now some relief was in sight: Bunches of icicles hung from the black overhang. However, I soon realized they were being plucked away by the climbers in front of Bonington and me, and few if any remained by the time we got on the pitch. As Bonington went up, I shouted for him to see if he could leave me one, which he did. But its small size and the effort it took to reach it canceled out most of the slight relief it gave my parched throat.

Moments like these stand out in my mind more than any of the technical difficulties of the climb. It was all the fuck-ups and lack of any real companionship and fun that made the climb more of an epic than the injury to MacInnes.

Above the overhang were some hard-to-protect slabs, and on one pitch I had to run it out in a diagonal line, which understandably upset Bonington, as a slip would have nearly landed him on the West Face route. He shouted curses up at me, but like a gentleman, he apologized when he reached the belay, muttering something about not behaving like an Army officer.

He led the next pitch, and near the end had to request a toprope from Whillans and MacInnes, who had found some ice, got the stove out, and were having their first real water for nearly three days. Bonington's request for a toprope was probably more due to dehydration and fatigue than difficulty. I could soon see Bonington having some mouthfuls of water and hear the hiss of the stove melting more ice. I rushed up the pitch, overcome with desperation to get water.

What happened next may now seem trivial, but I remember it as catastrophic. The pot of ice was all but melted; a few lumps floated on the surface. As I reached for it, Bonington said, "Wait until it is completely melted." I protested but he insisted. He then stood up, stumbled, and kicked the pot over. I could have cried as I watched the water drain into cracks in the rocks. It was now my turn to curse Bonington out. Worse, both Whillans and I had run out of cigarettes. It was a bloody nightmare.

Apparently, there was no time to melt any more ice, perhaps because there was no more ice on the ledge. Just before nightfall, somewhere below the actual summit of the Dru, we reached the end of the climb. It was cloudy and cold, but at least we now had some snow to melt, and we all shared a few mouthfuls of soup made from a packet that had managed to escape Whillans when two days earlier he had flung our food supply into the Dru Couloir.

It started to snow. I huddled up into a fetal position protected by my now-tattered plastic Pack-a-Mac. It was going to be another long night.

Part V: The Descent

The previous year the Austrians had climbed the West Face route and descended from our position, so we thought there would be no problem finding the way down. The abseiling technique in 1958 used a crossed sling with a 'biner and a loop pulled up over each leg. The rope was clipped into the 'biner and pulled over one shoulder—not the most comfortable setup and not easy with frozen hands. Between us we had three three-hundred-foot 9mm ropes.

The Austrians set off, leading the way down. At one point Philip had an extremely close call. He'd placed a sling around a spike of rock, threaded the abseil rope through it, and jumped off. The sling had come off the spike, and Philip vanished, presumably for good.

There was a thump and a shout; he had landed a few feet down in a deep snow-filled chimney, and fortunately had not bounced.

It was now snowing quite hard. Small spindrift avalanches came pouring down the grooves, visibility was nil, and things were getting a bit rough.

Sure enough, another serious problem materialized. The Austrians and MacInnes had abseiled down together and pulled their rope. Bonington and Whillans had thrown another rope and started down the same groove. Visibility was down to about thirty feet, so everyone was out of sight. After a while I could hear lots of shouting, so I took off down Bonington and Whillans's rope. Eventually I reached the source of the shouts. About forty feet down, in another groove that branched to the right, were MacInnes and the two Austrians. Blach was huddled up on a small ledge. MacInnes shouted that Blach was in really bad shape and wanted to be left to die. And, because they had pulled their abseil rope, Philip was going to have to climb back up the groove to reach our rope.

With spindrift pouring on my head and hanging with frozen hands on my shoulder abseil, there was nothing I could do to help. I could hear more shouts coming from Bonington and Whillans, somewhere below. I figured at least when Philip climbed out of their groove he would have this abseil rope in place. I continued down and nearly abseiled off the ends of the rope, which were hanging in space, away from the ledge that Bonington and Whillans had landed on. My hands frozen, I was losing my grip. As I tried to swing toward the ledge, I shouted at Bonington and Whillans to grab the ends of the rope and pull me over.

It now seemed to be every man for himself, and it soon got worse. I unclipped from the rope, and Whillans shouted at me to pull the rope down. I then told him what was happening above with MacInnes and the Austrians (actually, he must have seen their predicament when he abseiled), and that we should leave the rope and wait for them to use it. Once again he flew into a rage and screamed, "Pull the fucking rope!" It was now obvious what he was thinking—that is, "screw it, that's their problem and I am going to look after number one and that's me." I kept repeating "but what about . . ." but he just kept screaming "pull the fucking ropes." I recall Bonington saying that I had better pull the ropes. At this stage I was too tired to argue anymore, so I pulled.

As it turned out, it was only the strength of Philip that got them out of a very serious situation. Philip, belayed by MacInnes, who remarkably seemed to have completely recovered from the effects of his head injury, took two falls before he managed to climb out of their groove to where our rope had been. He then had to pull up MacInnes and a very weak Blach, and set up another abseil. They eventually caught up with us, and I remember MacInnes not being too pleased about us not leaving our rope in place for them. I am sure that if MacInnes had asked about it later, the finger of blame for the rope-pulling would've been attributed to me, which I guess was technically accurate.

A little farther down, MacInnes and I were descending a fairly steep snow slope. He was behind me with my North Wall hammer; I had nothing in my hands. Suddenly my footholds collapsed, and for a brief moment I thought, this is it. MacInnes, with his snow and ice skills, held me—not an easy catch, as we had been both moving together.

As we got lower on the mountain, it stopped snowing. Blach had recovered, and he and Philip were now a long way ahead, followed by Whillans and Bonington. I was now bringing up the rear with MacInnes. It seemed we had been designated the rope-pullers and carriers. Carrying three wet three-hundred-foot ropes and the rest of the gear was not easy after three days without food or much sleep. It now seemed that despite MacInnes being the weakest member of the group due to his bashed-in head, he had (with myself) been left with the hardest work of the descent.

As mentioned, we had three three-hundred-foot ropes. The system devised by the two groups in front was to throw down one abseil rope, descend it, then scramble down fairly easy ground to where another abseil was needed, then throw another rope down, and so on. The only time we saw the two groups ahead of us was when they ran out of ropes. Several times MacInnes and I had problems finding the route down, as after pulling and coiling ropes we would be well out of sight and sound of the others. We were both tired and getting pissed off with them never waiting to see if we were following okay.

This agitation came to a head when MacInnes and I came to another abseil point and down this one, for some unknown reason, were two of the three-hundred-foot ropes. The Austrians were nowhere in sight, but lying on their backs on a patch of snow several feet from the rope ends were Bonington and Whillans, relaxing and having a chitchat.

I thought, "fuck this." I was not about to let Whillans give Bonington lessons on how to become a lazy bugga. I slid down one of the ropes and marched down the snow slope toward them. They both looked surprised when I started to let them know how I felt: "You two lazy fuckers. I don't suppose you thought of at least pulling down one of these bloody ropes."

I stalked back up to the ropes. MacInnes and I pulled and coiled the ropes. The other two said nothing and, of course, did nothing. I felt better having let off a bit of steam. I was very impressed with MacInnes. He was a tough bloke and obviously a very reliable person to have around in sticky situations.

At last we reached the glacier and staggered down to the Charpoua hut. It was locked, but we managed to get inside and looked for food. No luck, but we at least now had lots of water. With nothing more than a long walk down the Mer de Glace, everyone seemed to gain new energy.

I must admit it felt great to be free and away from the company of Whillans and his surly tantrums. I took off with Blach down the glacier to the Montenvers railway station, running, laughing, and jumping the small, open crevasses. This was the first I had been alone with Riccardo, and although neither of us could understand each other's language, we were both happy to escape the tension of the previous four days.

We reached Montenvers way ahead of the others. The last train of the day to Chamonix was just about to leave. I knew the others were planning to eat at the Montenvers hotel, so I had to decide whether to stay or leave.

Two things prompted my departure. First, the friends from Carlisle that I traveled over with were leaving the next day, and they wouldn't know if I was okay before they left. Second, I couldn't stand another night with Whillans. I could have given up the chance to see my friends off, but the latter was just too much. Now that we were on level ground, I'm sure that one more word out of him would have involved more than us exchanging only curses.

I said goodbye to Riccardo and jumped on the train.

A REVIEW OF *DOWNWARD BOUND* (1975)

Royal Robbins

This book is a farce. And insofar as the success of a book is to be judged by the achievement of the author's intentions, *Downward Bound* must be judged a success. Its war cry repeated throughout is: *"Semper farcissmus!"* To take a cue from a film advertising cliché. Warren Harding is *Downward Bound*. And the book is distilled Harding.

Downward Bound was sent to me in galley-proof form by the editors of *Mountain Gazette*. I have reservations about writing a review from a galley proof. It isn't, after all, the finished product. There may be mistakes and absurdities caught by the reviewer which do not appear in the published work. And more than words make a book. The presentation is part of it—the paper size, binding, type, layout, drawings, and photographs. I assume that the finished product will be appropriate to the text.

The galleys arrived with the appendix in front. This seemed quite natural, because of what was in the appendix, and also because I wasn't surprised at Harding putting his book together ass-backwards. The appendix is, as a matter of fact, the best part of the book. I hope it remains in the front, because it provides a good introduction to what follows.

In this appendix, we are given a hierarchy of climbing levels, from one to ten. The white hats are at level one, and the hats slowly gray, becoming black at level ten, where we find "those blackguards, who climb for heathen reasons." Harding, of course, is at level ten. He likes to fancy himself the worst rascal around—no wishy-washy good guy, no second-rate bandit, but Billy the Kid himself. The generalized hierarchy is followed by vignette-like character sketches, as Harding assigns his numerous acquaintances, many of them well known in the little world of climbing, to their proper niches. For example:

"Tim Auger—Zone 8: This mild-mannered little fellow has compiled an impressive list of ascents as a result of his being included on strong American climbing teams as a 'token Canadian.'"

"Dean Caldwell—Zone 10: An archfiend of alpinism; set standards of despiciosity."

"Jim Bridwell—Zone 2: Head Kahuna of Yosemite's Camp 4 and is the founding director of the Jim Bridwell Memorial Rock Climbers' Gymnasium in Camp 4 olympic-training centre."

"Kim Schmitz—Zone 2: Similar to Jim Bridwell but not as handsome."

There are many more in the same vein. If Harding knows you, you may be there.

Harding has long been known, and feared, for his ability to see a person's weakness and sum it up savagely, to caricature. By contrast with what I have seen him do, the portraits here are almost loving. Anaïs Nin says in her diary, that it takes great hate to caricature. This book, though angry at times, seems to have been written in a generally benevolent mood.

Royal Robbins in 1994

After the portraits, we are treated to "Miscellaneous Inconsequential Bits of Climbing Information," which provide Harding another opportunity for satire, such as:

"Climbing Schools: Rock Craft (sic)—RR and his hairy giants provide rock-climbing instruction at any level that can be imagined and some that can't!" and "Climbing Journals: *Mountain*—Ken Wilson, the editor, is clearly insane! He is a veritable alpine Elmer Gantry."

Harding likes that last sentence. He used the identical words to refer to me in the 1971 issue of *Ascent*, in an article titled "Reflections of a Broken-Down Climber."

After the appendix, which provides a good introduction, comes "Acknowledgments," wherein Harding acknowledges lack of any knowledge of writing. "It may not sound classy, folks, but it's all me!" And so it is. In Harding's own words, the book is about ". . . twenty years of mountain experience, all those great people I've climbed with, eaten and drunk with, loved and hated, the mountains themselves, the good times and the bad."

The format is unusual, quite apart from the appendix. It's a story told as a slide-lecture program: "The Last Lecture Show," with an unusual cast of characters, among them Batso (Harding), Beasto—"a beautiful, talented young lady who, in a lapse of sanity, became romantically and professionally associated with the infamous Batso," a Martian, Dr. Sigmund Freud, and Penthouse Pundit (Ken Wilson).

In the preface, Harding promises to "shed some light on the fun and games known as rock climbing," a hint of his great (and healthy) contempt for all those who take climbing seriously, a contempt expressed again and again here in the

Harding's license plate in the early 1990s. "Al" refers to Alice Flomp, his partner of many years.

form of mockery of the climbing establishment, its organs, and its spokesmen.

The first section is "Act One—Climbing Information on How to Get Nowhere the Hard Way." This is a sort of manual explaining what rock climbing is and describing the equipment and how to climb rock. It is direct enough, though with numerous attempts at humor, not all of them successful. And there are a few oddities—for example: the definition of a peak as a summit; the statement that all climbing hammers have heads weighing about thirty-two ounces (some are half that), that runners are loops of one-inch nylon webbing (some are); Tahquitz is misspelled; and in discussing the high cost of climbing equipment, Harding quotes ropes at $50. It must have been a long time since Harding bought a climbing rope, as the current price is nearly twice that.

In this same section Harding ventures onto some thin ice without his crampons. He discusses the questions of ethics and morality in climbing and lambasts those who have truck with either. With much of this I am in agreement, especially with the instinct for anarchy (a healthy instinct, but best kept in bounds by "archy"). In one paragraph, he cleverly likens the "Puritan aversion to, and fear of, sex" and the "phobia concerning bolts"; he concludes that the fears of Chouinard and Robbins (that everyone will follow Harding's example of bolting blank walls) are exaggerated, because although everyone has become sex-happy, everyone won't become bolt-happy, since "screwing is more enjoyable than drilling bolt holes!"

Fair enough. But then he says a "bolt is simply one of the tools, and I attach no moral significance to its use." And later, "a climber who places bolts where pitons or other things would do just as well is simply wasting his time and is something of a fool." Well . . . who says A must equal B? Harding says the use of equipment is simply a question of efficiency. But on the *Wall of the Early Morning Light*, there were many places where the nailing was so difficult that it would have been faster to rivet. At five minutes per rivet (Harding's estimate), why was Harding wasting his time placing marginal pitons? In one case they were so marginal he took a forty-foot fall. Could it be he was playing the game of minimizing bolts—and was being "something of a fool"?

The second part of the book is more interesting. It's a brief history of Harding's climbing career, and a not-so-brief account of his biggest climb, "the Dawn Wall." The last is, indeed, the core of the book, and is described with a minimum of raving. It is the story of twenty-seven days on a twenty-eight-hundred-foot cliff, vertical or overhanging much of the way. Harding calls it "the Big Motha Climb." Harding and Caldwell showed a remarkable tenacity and toughness, more than has been shown by most climbers and by probably all of their detractors and critics. It was, in fact, a formidable effort. When Lauria and I made the second ascent in February 1971, I was impressed by two things. One was the quality of the aid work. Harding, by his own definition, may have been foolish to have wasted time avoiding rivets when the nailing got sticky, but the route is more challenging and of a higher quality because of it. The other thing was the difficulty of retreat. I had doubted that this was a genuine problem, but when we were about six hundred feet up, it came home to me with a chill, just how committed we were because of the overhanging nature of the rock. I was very pleased to have been spared the ordeal of fighting our way up through winter storms.

The aftermath has its high moments too. Harding is at his best when talking about other people—he's such a satirical rogue. One night he came to a party at my house, a booze party for climbers. His leg was still in a cast from running in front of a truck. He passed the evening standing on one leg—leaning against our kitchen counter—indulging in his favorite sport, and indeed, we were all drinking freely. He was in a nasty mood and stood there, picking us off one by one with slashing verbal attacks, startling in their power and trenchancy. I have never been put off by Harding's ravings, but this time the tone was so acid it put a damper on the party (a bit). Most of us were in bed by three, but Harding and Don Lauria argued until dawn.

But as I was saying, Harding is at his best when talking about people. Some of Caldwell's characteristics, which came out on the climb, startled Harding. And he was to be even more startled by some others, which evinced themselves in the aftermath. There was a rapid dissolution of their friendship because of Harding's aversion to Caldwell's avarice. Unusual stuff, bringing to mind the suit between Herrligkoffer and Messner.

Then there's the other part of the aftermath—the second ascent by Lauria and me and our ineffectual effort at "erasing" the route. Along with the applause for Harding's and Caldwell's achievement, there had been dismay on the part of many serious Yosemite climbers—dismay because they judged the route significantly more artificial than any other on El Capitan. This, because of bolts and rivets, accounted for a third of the progress. This seemed to many of us, and to me in particular, to be a foot in the door of a change pointing toward degradation of Yosemite climbing. We felt deeply that the sport of climbing has to have limits, and that these limits had been breached. Whether either of these judgments is true is a topic for a separate discussion. A number of climbers were vociferous in their indignation, but words were cheap compared with the twenty-seven days of action in which Harding lived out his own anarchic instincts. The only effective course was a countervailing action, which would make vivid the other side of the story. So I hit upon "erasing" the route as an expression of where I thought the line should be drawn. Of course, Lauria and I botched the job. But although Harding, in a sense, won by default, our message did get out, and there have been no more such escapades in Yosemite.

Considering Harding's ability to rage over comparative trifles, and that he was the injured party of our erasure scheme, his reaction, as expressed in his book, is mild and generally fair. He calls me an "alpine Carrie Nation," substituting hammer and chisel for hatchet and expansion bolts for whiskey bottles! (That's another of Harding's favorite phrases, culled from his article in *Ascent* for use in this book.) And he's got it nearly right. Unlike one of Harding's defenders (or my attackers), whose whole hysterical complaints envenomed the pages of *Mountain Gazette* a few issues back, Harding understands that, given his philosophy, we had as much right to remove the bolts as he to place them; and that given my philosophy, there was a temporary setting aside of the precept of leaving established routes alone so a large and pressing question could be battled out. The whole thing is passé, and a bit silly, but if one demands the right to place bolts as one pleases, the right to remove bolts as one pleases must be granted as well.

I might add that I am still in favor of leaving bolts in place, the exceptional circumstances of the Dawn Wall notwithstanding. When I was chopping those bolts I felt bad about doing it. It was as if I was hitting Harding with every blow, and I counted Harding among my friends (I still do). Our motives were quite different from those of the ace Yosemite aid man who made a subsequent ascent and chopped bolts he could pass without using. The same chap told me he intended to return and chop quite a few more bolts, the better to remake the route in his own image. Such bolt chopping is merely a way of underlining one's own superiority, and shows ruthless contempt for the work of other men.

Aside from occasional flashes of humor, insight, and character delineation, there are generalizations that ring true, such as:

"I've never really understood what's supposed to be so bad about climbs receiving publicity. I don't believe the majority of climbers feel it is undesirable. It seems to me more of a snob thing among the elite who have come to believe that (presumably, because they climb rocks) they are some sort of superior breed, who should remain above the public view and that climbing must retain a mystical esoteric image."

That's a fair statement.

But a lot of the writing is pretty terrible. And there is some false sentiment (a very hard thing to avoid). Like all passionate climbers, Harding is a romantic. He strives for the impossible. And he fancies himself all bad. He takes pride in wearing the black hat, and he likes to picture himself as drunkenness, gluttony, sloth, cowardice, treachery, lechery, and avarice incarnate. Drunken, but he has no claim to other sins. Harding can be demonic, but he is not as much of a devil as he likes to think. He is anything but lazy (though he may be indolent for brief spells). He is clearly not a coward (he may at times be afraid, but he does things a man paralyzed by fear can scarcely imagine). No one has ever suggested that Harding is not loyal to his friends, but his generosity, even under duress, has been commented upon. Most important, Harding is honest. His main aim, his obsession, has been to climb the "Ultimate Rock Wall." Doing big walls gives him a sort of peace. I think he likes the gaze of the public—but so what? I, for one, have had a bellyfull of those exquisite moralists who complain constantly about minor human vices. That's certainly not the reason he climbs, even if it is a corollary of his climbing impulse. Harding climbs primarily for the satisfaction of achievement. Everything else is secondary. He doesn't elevate his own importance by talking down the achievements of others. And he would never step on a piton and forget about it and say he had done it free. Because what is most important to him is what he does.

Though not the bad hombre he romantically pictures himself to be, Harding is an hombre. He keeps his integrity and gives the finger to the world. His cussedness and orneriness are virtues. In a climbing world becoming ever more gray and homogenized, Harding stands out as a richly colorful character. We wouldn't want too many Hardings around, but a few more like him would be all to the good.

As an "insider," I found the book interesting. What others will think is hard to guess, but I doubt if Prentice-Hall will sell many copies. I hope I'm wrong, and perhaps I will be. After all, who would have predicted that the doughty dude who climbed the *Wall of the Early Morning Light* would have briefly become one of the most sought-after celebrities of American climbing history?

THE ASCENT OF MONT VENTOUX (1336)

Francesco Petrarch

Today I made the ascent of the highest mountain in this region, which is not improperly called Ventosum. My only motive was the wish to see what so great an elevation had to offer. I have had the expedition in mind for many years; for, as you know, I have lived in this region from infancy, having been cast here by that fate which determines the affairs of men. Consequently the mountain, which is visible from a great distance, was ever before my eyes, and I conceived the plan of sometime doing what I have at last accomplished today. The idea took hold upon me with especial force when, in rereading Livy's *History of Rome* yesterday, I happened upon the place where Philip of Macedon, the same who waged war against the Romans, ascended Mount Haemus in Thessaly, from whose summit he was able, it is said, to see two seas, the Adriatic and the Euxine. Whether this be true or false I have not been able to determine, for the mountain is too far away, and writers disagree. Pomponius Mela, the cosmographer—not to mention others who have spoken of this occurrence—admits its truth without hesitation; Titus Livius, on the other hand, considers it false. I, assuredly, should not have left the question long in doubt, had that mountain been as easy to explore as this one. Let us leave this matter to one side, however, and return to my mountain here—it seems to me that a young man in private life may well be excused for attempting what an aged king could undertake without arousing criticism.

When I came to look about for a companion, I found, strangely enough, that hardly one among my friends seemed suitable, so rarely do we meet with just the right combination of personal tastes and characteristics, even among those who are dearest to us. This one was too apathetic, that one overanxious; this one too slow, that one too hasty; one was too sad, another overcheerful; one more simple, another more sagacious, than I desired. I feared this one's taciturnity and that one's loquacity. The heavy deliberation of some repelled me as much as the lean incapacity of others. I rejected those who were likely to irritate me by a cold want of interest, as well as those who might weary me by their excessive enthusiasm. Such defects, however grave, could be borne with at home, for charity suffereth all things, and friendship accepts any burden; but it is quite otherwise on a journey, where every weakness becomes much more serious. So, as I was bent upon pleasure and anxious that my enjoyment should be unalloyed, I looked about me with unusual care, balanced against one another the various characteristics of my friends, and without committing any breach of friendship I silently condemned every trait which might prove disagreeable on the way. And—would you believe it?—I finally turned homeward for aid, and proposed the ascent to my only brother, who is younger than I, and with whom you are well acquainted. He was delighted and gratified beyond measure by the thought of holding the place of a friend as well as of a brother.

At the time fixed we left the house, and by evening reached Malaucene, which lies at the foot of the mountain, to the north. Having rested there a day, we finally made the ascent this morning, with no companions except two servants; and a most difficult task it was. The mountain is a very steep and almost inaccessible mass of stony soil. But, as the poet has well said, "Remorseless toil conquers all." It was a long day, the air fine. We enjoyed the advantages of vigour of mind and strength and agility of body, and everything else essential to those engaged in such an undertaking, and so had no other difficulties to face than those of the region itself.

We found an old shepherd in one of the mountain dales, who tried, at great length, to dissuade us from the ascent, saying that some fifty years before he had, in the same ardour of youth, reached the summit, but had gotten for his pains nothing except fatigue and regret, and clothes and body torn by the rocks and briars. No one, so far as he or his companions knew, had ever tried the ascent before or after him. But his counsels increased rather than diminished our desire to proceed, since youth is suspicious of warnings. So the old man, finding that his efforts were in vain, went a little way with us, and pointed out a rough path among the rocks, uttering many admonitions, which he continued to send after us even after we had left him behind.

Surrendering to him all such garments or other possessions as might prove burdensome to us, we made ready for the ascent, and started off at a good pace. But, as usually happens, fatigue quickly followed upon our excessive exertion, and we soon came to a halt at the top of a certain cliff. Upon starting on again we went more slowly, and I especially advanced along the rocky way with a more deliberate step. While my brother chose a direct path straight up the ridge, I weakly took an easier one which really descended. When I was called back, and the right road was shown me; I replied that I hoped to find a better way round on the other side, and that I did not mind going farther if the path were only less steep. This was just an excuse for my laziness; and when the others had already reached a considerable height I was still wandering in the valleys. I had failed to find an easier path, and had only increased the distance and difficulty of the ascent.

At last I became disgusted with the intricate way I had chosen, and resolved to ascend without more ado. When I reached my brother, who, while waiting for me, had had ample opportunity for rest, I was tired and irritated. We walked along together for a time, but hardly had we passed the first spur when I forgot about the circuitous route which I had just tried, and took a lower one again. Once more I followed an easy, roundabout path through winding valleys, only to find myself soon in my old difficulty. I was simply trying to avoid the exertion of the ascent; but no human ingenuity can alter the nature of things, or cause anything to reach a height by going down. Suffice it to say that, much to my vexation and my brother's amusement, I made this same mistake three times or more during a few hours.

After being frequently misled in this way, I finally sat down in a valley and transferred my winged thoughts from things corporeal to the immaterial, addressing myself as follows: "What thou hast repeatedly experienced today in the ascent of this mountain, happens to thee, as to many, in the journey toward the blessed life. But this is not so readily perceived by men, since the motions of the body are obvious and external while those of the soul are invisible and hidden.

Yes, the life which we call blessed is to be sought for on a high eminence, and straight is the way that leads to it. Many, also, are the hills that lie between, and we must ascend, by a glorious stairway, from strength to strength. At the top is at once the end of our struggles and the goal for which we are bound. All wish to reach this goal, but, as Ovid says, 'To wish is little; we must long with the utmost eagerness to gain our end.' Thou certainly dost ardently desire, as well as simply wish, unless thou deceivest thyself in this matter, as in so many others. What, then, doth hold thee back? Nothing, assuredly, except that thou wouldst take a path which seems, at first thought, more easy, leading through low and worldly pleasures. But nevertheless in the end, after long wanderings, thou must perforce either climb the steeper path, under the burden of tasks foolishly deferred, to its blessed culmination, or lie down in the valley of thy sins, and (I shudder to think of it!), if the shadow of death overtake thee, spend an eternal night amid constant torments."

These thoughts stimulated both body and mind in a wonderful degree for facing the difficulties which yet remained. Oh, that I might traverse in spirit that other road for which I long day and night, even as today I overcame material obstacles by my bodily exertions! And I know not why it should not be far easier, since the swift immortal soul can reach its goal in the twinkling of an eye, without passing through space, while my progress today was necessarily slow, dependent as I was upon a failing body weighed down by heavy members.

One peak of the mountain, the highest of all, the country people call "Sonny," why, I do not know, unless by antiphrasis, as I have sometimes suspected in other instances; for the peak in question would seem to be the father of all the surrounding ones. On its top is a little level place, and here we could at last rest our tired bodies.

Now, my father, since you have followed the thoughts that spurred me on in my ascent, listen to the rest of the story, and devote one hour, I pray you, to reviewing the experiences of my entire day. At first, owing to the unaccustomed quality of the air and the effect of the great sweep of view spread out before me, I stood like one dazed. I beheld the clouds under our feet, and what I had read of Athos and Olympus seemed less incredible as I myself witnessed the same things from a mountain of less fame. I turned my eyes toward Italy, whither my heart most inclined. The Alps, rugged and snow-capped, seemed to rise close by, although they were really at a great distance; the very same Alps through which that fierce enemy of the Roman name once made his way, bursting the rocks, if we may believe the report, by the application of vinegar. I sighed, I must confess, for the skies of Italy, which I beheld rather with my mind than with my eyes. An inexpressible longing came over me to see once more my friend and my country. At the same time I reproached myself for this double weakness, springing, as it did, from a soul not yet steeled to manly resistance. And yet there were excuses for both of these cravings, and a number of distinguished writers might be summoned to support me.

Then a new idea took possession of me, and I shifted my thoughts to a consideration of time rather than place. "Today it is ten years since, having completed thy youthful studies, thou didst leave Bologna. Eternal God! In the name of immutable wisdom, think what alterations in thy character this intervening period has beheld! I pass over a thousand instances. I am not yet in a safe harbour where I can calmly recall past storms. The time may come when I can review in due order all the experiences of the past, saying with St. Augustine, 'I desire to recall my foul actions and the carnal corruption of my soul, not because I love them, but that I may the more love thee, O my God.' Much that is doubtful and evil still clings to me, but what I once loved, that I love no longer. And yet what am I saying? I still love it, but with shame, but with heaviness of heart. Now, at last, I have confessed the truth. So it is. I love, but love what I would not love, what I would that I might hate. Though loath to do so, though constrained, though sad and sorrowing, still I do love, and I feel in my miserable self the truth of the well-known words, 'I will hate if I can; if not, I will love against my will.' Three years have not yet passed since that perverse and wicked passion which had a firm grasp upon me and held undisputed sway in my heart began to discover a rebellious opponent, who was unwilling longer to yield obedience. These two adversaries have joined in close combat for the supremacy, and for a long time now a harassing and doubtful war has been waged in the field of my thoughts."

Thus I turned over the last ten years in my mind, and then, fixing my anxious gaze on the future, I asked myself, "If, perchance, thou shouldst prolong this uncertain life of thine for yet two lustres, and shouldst make an advance toward virtue proportionate to the distance to which thou hast departed from thine original infatuation during the past two years, since the new longing first encountered the old, couldst thou, on reaching thy fortieth year, face death, if not with complete assurance, at least with hopefulness, calmly dismissing from thy thoughts the residuum of life as it faded into old age?"

These and similar reflections occurred to me, my father. I rejoiced in my progress, mourned my weaknesses, and commiserated the universal instability of human conduct. I had well-nigh forgotten where I was and our object in coming; but at last I dismissed my anxieties, which were better suited to other surroundings, and resolved to look about me and see what we had come to see. The sinking sun and the lengthening shadows of the mountain were already warning us that the time was near at hand when we must go. As if suddenly wakened from sleep, I turned about and gazed toward the west. I was unable to discern the summits of the Pyrenees, which form the barrier between France and Spain; not because of any intervening obstacle that I know of but owing simply to the insufficiency of our mortal vision. But I could see with the utmost clearness, off to the right, the mountains of the region about Lyons, and to the left the bay of Marseilles and the waters that lash the shores of Aigues Mortes, altho' all these places were so distant that it would require a journey of several days to reach them. Under our very eyes flowed the Rhone.

While I was thus dividing my thoughts, now turning my attention to some terrestrial object that lay before me, now raising my soul, as I had done my body, to higher planes, it occurred to me to look into my copy of St. Augustine's *Confessions*, a gift that I owe to your love, and that I always have about me, in memory of both the author and the giver. I opened the compact little volume, small indeed in size but of infinite charm, with the intention of reading whatever came to hand, for I could happen upon nothing that would be otherwise than edifying and devout. Now it chanced that the tenth book presented itself.

My brother, waiting to hear something of St. Augustine's from my lips, stood attentively by. I call him, and God too, to witness that where I first fixed my eyes it was written: "And men go about to wonder at the heights of the mountains, and the mighty waves of the sea, and the wide sweep of rivers, and the circuit of the ocean, and the revolution of the stars, but themselves they consider not." I was abashed, and, asking my brother (who was anxious to hear more) not to annoy me, I closed the book, angry with myself that I should still be admiring earthly things who might long ago have learned from even the pagan philosophers that nothing is wonderful but the soul, which, when great itself, finds nothing great outside itself. Then, in truth, I was satisfied that I had seen enough of the mountain; I turned my inward eye upon myself, and from that time not a syllable fell from my lips until we reached the bottom again.

Those words had given me occupation enough, for I could not believe that it was by a mere accident that I happened upon them. What I had there read I believed to be addressed to me and to no other, remembering that St. Augustine had once suspected the same thing in his own case, when, on opening the book of the Apostle, as he himself tells us, the first words that he saw there were, "Not in rioting and drunkenness, not in chambering and wantonness, not in strife and envying. But put ye on the Lord Jesus Christ, and make not provision for the flesh, to fulfil the lusts thereof."

The same thing happened earlier to St. Anthony, when he was listening to the Gospel where it is written, "If thou wilt be perfect, go and sell that thou hast, and give to the poor, and thou shalt have treasure in heaven: and come and follow me." Believing this scripture to have been read for his special benefit, as his biographer Athanasius says, he guided himself by its aid to the Kingdom of Heaven. And as Anthony on hearing these words waited for nothing more, and as Augustine upon reading the Apostle's admonition sought no further, so I concluded my reading in the few words which I had given.

I thought in silence of the lack of good counsel in us mortals, who neglect what is noblest in ourselves, scatter our energies in all directions, and waste ourselves in a vain show, because we look about us for what is to be found only within. I wondered at the natural nobility of our soul, save when it debases itself of its own free will, and deserts its original estate, turning what God has given it for its honour into dishonour. How many times, think you, did I turn back that day, to glance at the summit of the mountain which seemed scarcely a cubit high compared with the range of human contemplation—when it is not immersed in the foul mire of Earth? With every downward step I asked myself this: If we are ready to endure so much sweat and labour in order that we may bring our bodies a little nearer Heaven, how can a soul struggling toward God, up the steeps of human pride and human destiny, fear any cross or prison or sting of fortune? How few, I thought, but are diverted from their path by the fear of difficulties or the love of ease! How happy the lot of those few, if any such there be! It is of them, assuredly, that the poet was thinking, when he wrote:

Happy the man who is skilled to understand Nature's hid causes;
who beneath his feet
All terrors casts, and death's relentless doom,
And the loud roar of greedy Acheron.

How earnestly should we strive, not to stand on mountaintops, but to trample beneath us those appetites which spring from earthly impulses.

With no consciousness of the difficulties of the way, amidst these preoccupations which I have so frankly revealed, we came, long after dark, but with the full moon lending us its friendly light, to the little inn which we had left that morning before dawn. The time during which the servants have been occupied in preparing our supper, I have spent in a secluded part of the house, hurriedly jotting down these experiences on the spur of the moment, lest, in case my task were postponed, my mood should change on leaving the place, and so my interest in writing flag.

You will see, my dearest father, that I wish nothing to be concealed from you, for I am careful to describe to you not only my life in general but even my individual reflections. And I beseech you, in turn, to pray that these vague and wandering thoughts of mine may some time become firmly fixed, and, after having been vainly tossed about from one interest to another, may direct themselves at last toward the single, true, certain, and everlasting good.

Malaucene, April 26 [1336]

FREAKERS' BALL (1974)

Jeff Salz

October 20

A yellow Ford barrels past pigtailed ladies in great skirts and bowler hats. Old barefooted men move their oxen along in first light. A bright flock of flamingos takes to the air from a green reed pond. Across the Peruvian highlands we scatter Indians and stray dogs, churning up road dust that covers our hair and pastes our eyes. We are the Freakers' Ball bound for a mountain called FitzRoy in Argentine Patagonia, not daring to focus our minds on our objective for the very power of our dreams.

November 1

Days of nonstop driving have brought us to Calafate, Agentina, the true capital of Patagonia. Doña Rosa is our *mamacita*, her hotel our home. In an old housedress, with a toothpick in her mouth, she remembers Toni Egger, who died on Cerro Torre. "Oh, that little one, he is still up there, *pobrecito*, how he could eat." It is the land of the gaucho, the *peón*, the *patrón*, calloused hands and quiet kindness. FitzRoy looms among the clouds, past the lakes, ferries, and mud holes to the north. Ostrich scurry, guanaco leap, and everywhere wander the sheep.

A day's travel brings us to the end of the road. Sleeping bags are laid down beneath dreary skies. In the morning we totter sleepily from the warmth of our bags and stand, each alone, gazing at the towers which stand suddenly revealed against a miraculously clear sky. Our minds are open and our hearts too. Patagonia—cold and dreadful, glorious and beautiful. We have learned that here a mountaineer's hopes always border on illusion. Reckless dreams are of a blue sky that may never be seen. There is toil and trouble, all probably in vain. But if the awaited day does arrive, you can stop shivering and rejoice, for there are few days like it in a lifetime. And when your luck fails and you depart with sadness, there is the wonder at how much was gained by all the discomfort and hard times. Finally, after the farewell, a stirring in your heart grows recognizable as that forlorn hope coming round one more time, daring you to come back.

We are on our way to base camp with the first loads of six weeks of rations. In shorts we cross meadows of dandelions and sunshine. Packs are weighted down with books, bongs, stoves, and salami. We cross rivers and move through forests of linga trees and shadows; all the while reigning above us is FitzRoy. The mountain has come to symbolize for us an ultimate quest. It is as vital to us and as holy as any place on Earth. In our lives there is no place we would rather be. Now we actually find ourselves here. For any mountaineer this is the big time. I'm not surprised to find myself as nervous as a leaf.

November 3

Kelty fully loaded, I am a human offering to the wind. Careening sideways up and down glacial moraines spun like a top, I am as helpless as a kitten. It takes a day and a half to reach the shanty that will be our base camp. Kevin is here;

Fitzroy from the east

the rest have gone back for another load. It seems we will be able to do the whole thing without guides or horses. Our shelter is an airy cabin of logs and biscuit tins, with leisurely improvements made by a decade of expeditions waiting out storms. Rain patters on the tin roofing. It is the end of the day and I am homesick, slightly more confident, and exhausted. Time for sleep.

November 3

The weather blows and snows. It is evening, in the cabin, by the fire. Two days ago Kevin and I, heading westward toward the glacier on a reconnaissance, were halted by a whiteout and enjoyed a small epic trying to cross a thin, mossy ledge covered by slippery snow. We escaped unscathed, of course. Today, while grunting back to base camp under the last load, including food and tape recorder, I fell into the river. Thoroughly soaked, I decided expeditions are not a fun pastime.

November 7

It will be Kevin and Dave, and Steve and me, on the climb, New Zealand and North American teams. Two ropes of two, climbing alpine style; that's the way our expedition must climb FitzRoy. Noel is here working. Randy and Bill have done more load carrying than anyone else, and since they will not be doing the actual climb, have gone fishing. Steve and Kevin are off to dig a snow cave at the base of our route, the *Super Couloir*. The weather is calming down, and with the trials of the epic still ahead, it is peaceful in the cabin tonight.

I have my doubts whether I shall even stand atop FitzRoy. I recall the night I sat in concentration upon the grass mat

in our house in the Peruvian Andes. The candlelight flick-
ered as I tossed the coins for a reading of the *I Ching*. The
book told an offering and did not speak of success. My eyes
clouded with tears of presentiment. But now we are here and
must put everything we can into the effort. Still, I must ask
myself what I am doing, and for whom.

The sheepskin rug feels good under my feet. The wind
tosses the treetops. David and I have our work cut out join-
ing Kevin and Steve on the glacier tomorrow with loads of
hardware. Though I would love to do this climb in a week
and be safely home for Thanksgiving, I am prepared for
at least a month and half of waiting. It all depends on the
weather . . . and me.

November 8–11

We are up at daybreak and every star is twinkling. Steve and I
eat our oatmeal and are off. It is four in the afternoon before
we have climbed the glacier with our loads and stand below
the climb. Already we are tired. Steve has been shouting
encouragement all day to help keep me up. The climb is so
foreshortened; I do not believe at first that we are beneath the
actual route. Noel, Kevin, and David are a few hours behind
us. It is perfectly calm and clear, without a breath of wind
from the ice cap. The gear is chosen and the climb begins. At
nine-thirty, in the last glow of day, we are still plugging away
in the soft snow, kicking steps. As the others appear below, we
yell, "A piece of duff!" The climb looks so easy, the summit
already within reach. Numb fingers pull me up through the
dark to a possible bivouac ledge. God, I'm glad to be climbing with Steve. From police station floors to sweaty shearing
sheds, I have never shared so trustingly with another soul. I

know I can depend on him, especially on a mountain where he knows how to move with safety and grace.

We step about like interior decorators upon a sloping ledge hardly enough to stand on. All we need now is to decide where to huddle for the night. Bundled into my parka, I wait for the rising of the moon and drop into fitful naps. Reluctantly the night gives way to the first rays of dawn. Down below, Kevin and David begin to climb. My boots were too far away during the night and have frozen solid. They only begin to thaw as they thud into hard ice.

Amid the activity hours pass like minutes, unnoticed. To arrive atop FitzRoy does not allow us to dwell on hunger or fatigue. We operate in a state above the physical, absorbed by a dream. Above the ice, the first rock section is an awkward crack led by Steve. The Kiwis are below us, so we leave the rope hanging and suspend everything, including ourselves, for lunch. We discuss salami skins and technocracies until the four of us are hanging together. More of Steve's leads follow while I carry the pack, jumaring and cleaning the protection. I wonder if I am doing my share. I ought to be doing more of the leading, but Steve is better at it than I will ever be. Seconding is not really climbing. Dehydration and thirst set in; pressing blistered lips to thawing ice I tear off hunks that only increase my desire for water. Warming sunshine reminds me of fair-weather climbing at home in the Prescott dells. Ascending the ropes over rough rock tears my knuckles to shreds. We are climbing in darkness, unable to find a bivouac ledge. No, nothing here either. One more pitch, though, and we are bound to find something. We settle upon two ledges like sloping school bus steps. I am exhausted. This wall just keeps going on up with never a place to lie down or even sit. All my gear hangs from me where I am pegged into a wall. I am tired of dangling in suspense and waiting for the storm that will come hurtling across the ice cap. The secure, commonplace domestic ways I have scorned appear overwhelmingly attractive from this perspective. There is no one up here to cradle me tonight. Trying to battle dizzying insecurity, I close my mind and retreat inward.

Steve is worse off, justifiably. He has done all the leading on the rock, and we have begun going light on rations. His voice is weak as he asks me to take care of him tonight. I loan him my parka while David and Kevin haul his pack from below. It jams tightly, beyond sight, and won't budge. This is awful. I find myself saying, "I'll go down and get it." No one is anxious to mess around with anchors, Jumars, and carabiners when in the dark and past exhaustion. It is a perfect setup for a tragic error. Rappelling into the darkness I force a weary brain to keep cranking for a few more stressful minutes. The pack is freed and I am back. Now I have done more than pull pitons; I am doing my part and I know I am needed.

Kevin has melting snow for soup, but the only place to rest the stove is on Dave's knee. Sploosh! He has fallen asleep. Wedging in I find myself upon a pinnacle that conveniently skewers my backside and solves the ever-present slidy sleeping slippage problem. Steve and I cover ourselves with a light orange sleeping tent, our heads emerging from matching wind tunnels. We must appear like vermillion, bearded, Siamese twin tortoises lodged on the wall of a mountain. I take over the cooking and stay awake long enough to hand out a cup of soup and a cup of tea each.

Day three, and rocks and snow continue to whiz by like giant wasps. In the Super Couloir, nothing looks steep, yet pitches tend to wind up as overhangs. I lead the first pitch with frozen feet and aching muscles. My body is rigid, my fingers are weak; two nights out make a debilitating difference. I use my knees a lot, trying to keep my grunting low. As a group of four we proceed slowly and only complete a few leads all day. Time sneaks by us. It is only a few pitches to the summit ridge and easier climbing, but we are very low on food and a storm is moving across the ice cap. We jam ourselves together for another night. I shiver inside my parka for countless hours anticipating the dawn. Finally, I grow impatient. "What time is it now?" I ask Dave. "Eleven-thirty" is the answer.

Snow patters upon our cagoules as a cloud engulfs our ledge, I sit awake, still. Steve is crushing my gonads but I say nothing; perhaps he is asleep. My mind races. As a group of four we are moving too slowly. The food is almost exhausted. A team of two can climb faster, take all the remaining food and be on top in a day even if the storm lasts. Before the climb we knew that Kevin and Steve would be the ones to reach the summit. In Peru even the *I Ching* had forecast their success, while telling David in no uncertain language "not to strive upward," but rather "to remain below." I was told of an offering and of a decision: "Full of trust they look to him." I will make a suggestion and it will be carried out. Two only can go on; it is best that it be one from each party. Of the Americans it must be Steven—he has climbed as hard and as well as any of us. David and I will descend. It seems that sacrificing the chance to stand atop FitzRoy will be my offering. Steve and Kevin will do the climb for all of us. The decision sits well with us; the good wind that guides the way.

Early in the morning I place the first pin and we begin our descent. We know we have come close, and when the sun breaks through it is difficult to head downward, but it's a little easier as the clouds roll in and the rock vanishes in mist. Rappel after rappel, my mind grows as worn as the rope . . . coils made and thrown . . . the rope is threaded through the sling . . . waist loop unclipped from the anchor and reclipped into a confusing carabiner brake system.

Down the rope I curse at the knots all gnarled and jammed in an intentional and malicious way. At the end of the rope I tie off and swing about in search of another piton place. The pin is barely satisfactory, but it will hold. A sling is threaded through the anchor and I clip into it. "Okay, Dave," I yell, and the whole damned business begins again. Sometimes one of us will forget the procedure and can only follow orders. After twenty full-length rappels we lose count. The weather remains mild, the storm undelivered, but the couloir has become a waterfall. My carabiner system effectively wrings the rope dry during each rappel and pours freezing water into my innocent crotch.

The rope jams behind some ice high above. Freeing it necessitates a serious climb. "Do you mind getting it, Dave, I'm exhausted."

"I'm exhausted too, and I got the last one."

He's right. I do it.

Ever downward as rocks whir by. Every nut, pin, and screw holds perfectly. Not a thought is wasted on the worth of all the equipment being left behind. We descend through rushing water where the hateful rope twists into horrible messes to be unraveled by trembling fingers. The rope is nearly worn through as the final rappel sets us on top of the soft snow in the lower section of the couloir. We belay, timidly kicking down through slick slush. Two figures can be seen waiting on the glacier. We are almost down now, glissading and running. We are almost down. A person is coming toward us. Dave leaps the final bergschrund and lands joyfully. He stops.

"Let's go, David!" I yell.

"I can't. My bloody leg is caught in the snow!"

How ridiculous. He pulls, grunts, moans, digs furiously, and at last is free.

We leap together. On waterlogged bottoms we toboggan madly down the slope, plowing up great masses of snow between our legs. YAHOOOO! Ecstasy. I totter into Randy's waiting arms. It is so good to see him, to touch him. Bill is there too, with candy and cheese. Salted peanuts burn my mouth. Body clasps and questions. Do we want to sleep in the snow cave tonight? Not on your life; let's make it back to the cabin. We rope up and Randy leads us across the glacier in the twilight. It is good to have friends like these to follow. We stumble beyond tiredness through the teetering boulders of the moraine. On and on we go, bruised and reeling drunkenly in the blackness.

At last there is a light through the trees. Trees, a miracle in themselves, fellow living things, give shelter. I press my face close to the bark of one and embrace it. Good old tree. Candlelight glimmers off the familiar biscuit-tin door. Randy has raced ahead and gotten the tea on. I step through the door into a room filled with the warmth of a flickering fire. It is two in the morning. God I feel good.

November 12

Success. Randy and Bill have returned to the base of the climb. The weather is superb. Everything tells me that they will climb it, and therefore that we will all have climbed it. But not until one of them tells me to my face will I totally believe it. It is a great thing for us all.

Why? Do I now understand why this is all so important?

Our efforts are symbolic, vital, and glorious. I have been alternately drained and exalted by the wonder of life. I didn't make it to the top; I made a difficult decision in keeping with the truth and knowledge within me. I have reached for an ultimate hope and tried my hardest and now, momentarily or forever, I am wholly at peace. Content within my thoughts, I sit quietly by the river in the sunshine. My body, aching and battered, feels wonderful on the grass. It is a good and lazy feeling of contentment and fulfillment. May the memory linger forever.

November 13, morning

The sky is full of wind and rain, and I worry and dream of Steve and Kevin out in the bad weather. FitzRoy assumes astounding dimensions in a nightmare and I wake up in a sweat, clutching my sleeping bag around me. The storms have come with no concern for the lives of mortal men. I spent yesterday relaxing in the sun, shoeless and shirtless. I am back in safety, but where are Kevin and Steve? Bill and Randy are still up at the mountain, waiting. I look back at all the insignificant mistakes we made: moving too slowly, going too light on rations. I am uneasy in my sleeping bag. I know this is not a usual day.

November 13, evening

Something dreadful has happened. We sit, four of us, in front of the pickup truck, doors barred against the flood. Music plays on the tape deck. We hum along, trying to forget that we have sunken so deep that if we open the doors the murky water will come flooding in, maybe drowning us completely. We are alone and helpless in a muddy pothole in the middle of the Argentine pampa.

Emptiness.

Steve has died. That is all there is. It puts all these words and every care into the ludicrous. Steve is dead, so is Kevin. There was a rockfall on the mountain.

It makes no sense so I don't really believe it. It is not possible that our golden expedition can end like this. We have lived in a world of good karma and happy endings, and now this has happened. If this is reality, it is not easy for me to understand. We are on our way to civilization to find a helicopter to get the bodies out. Skidding through the mud, we are laughing and working together much like before. Minus two.

It is crazy.

This morning the porridge was heating in the fireplace. The cabin was tidied for the triumphant return of the summit team. It was hard but I knew they had done it. The tape recorder was readied for the important story. They will be back any minute. Haven't we done a fine job?

There is something outside the cabin, people with backpacks. "Here come the boys," says Noel. I rush out, questions and congratulations on my lips. Randy is outside with Bill.

"We found their bodies at the foot of the couloir this morning." His eyes are wild.

I feel no pain, not like I'm supposed to. What is all this about? What is one supposed to do? Obviously Randy and Bill are shaken up, need comforting. They are alive, so I ask them to come inside and have some porridge. Steve and Kevin are friends and good climbers, not people who die on mountains. We dare death and use it as a tool to better know our lives, but we know our stuff and never succumb to it. It is not supposed to happen this way. I was all ready for the victory celebration and homeward flight. We have miraculously landed on our feet from every window we have fallen through. Now this.

Bill stays in the cabin; the rest of us begin the walk out. My thoughts are random and unchanneled, not mourning or laughing. I guess I can have the harmonica and the new Kelty ... how can I think things like this ... look at those geese fluttering on that pond, I guess they are Kevin and Steve. Our minds are blown, but we must arrive at the truck, eat, and go for help. Wheels skid and slip as we blast madly through each mud hole. Nothing can halt our mission now. We must get through. But one mud hole is too deep and we sink past the floorboards, immobile and wholly impotent. Wind howls at the truck and night comes.

November 15

Two freaks with a yellow briefcase walk into the Government House of Santa Cruz and the office swings into action. We are given coffee doubles, forms in triplicate, and sympathy in whispers. Typewriters clack amid a bustle and buzz. They will petition the federal government for a helicopter. Everyone scurries. More coffee arrives on silver trays carried by white-jacketed waiters. Elegant accommodations and dinners are courtesy of the Catholic Church. Steve and Kevin would be as amazed as we are. I think how glad I am that I was not the one who fell off FitzRoy.

David and I are being treated royally and are having a fine time.

Sometimes there is a frightening chill upon me. I think of the evil spirit the Indians said would cause tragedy when the clouds enveloped the summit. Are there demons and devils, Stephen? Is this death a frightening thing? If only you could tell me. Your death is so easily mine, and in death, as in life, you are showing me so much.

Telephone. I zoom down the marble hallway in my socks. It is the governor; the helicopter is on its way from Buenos Aires. Triumph.

Kevin's mom wants him buried here, close to the mountains. Typewriters clack. The American Counsel tells me from his office in B.A., "One thing we do have for Americans here in Argentina is a good funeral parlor."

David and I are in Rio Gallegos, Argentina, heralded and celebrated. Radio interviews. Free ice cream from a sympathetic grocer (we had it figured out early and ordered two scoops). An old English lady with her shopping bags asks, "Why did you leave your friends up there in the mountains?"

"They're dead, lady," says Dave.

Inside we are still very tender. We do not want to forget; we want only to learn. There is power in me, for I am the survivor. But for how long will I survive? And until then it has to be all, every last bit all the time, all that is the best of me. That I owe Steve and myself. FitzRoy is one way for a good man to go down. Because to live without a sing and a dance is not to live at all, really.

November 20

In the pioneer town of Calafate the dirt roads are swept by

dust devils. Men walk the streets slouching forward under caps pressed low. It takes a strong will to thrive in Patagonia. Soon all this will be a memory to me and no more. In the courtyard a turkey laughs. The sheriff says the rescue operation has the bodies. Doña Rosa says the sheriff does not know very much.

I dreamed last night that Steve was back, putting books on a library shelf. "But, Steve, I thought . . ."

"Shhhh . . . ," says Noel.

"Ohhh . . ." I begin to catch on. I do not want to botch it. We are going to extricate ourselves from yet another seemingly inescapable expedition crisis, as we have always done. Right, I can play it cool. Inevitably, curiosity gets the better of me. "Steven, aren't you the least bit sore or stiff or something?" He is okay. Really.

Question: Why do people climb mountains in Patagonia? Answer: It is too windy for marbles.

And perhaps because mountaineering here is of life, of the soul and spirit. It is a unique experience for each of us. Competitive journals and grading systems can go to hell. FitzRoy is only a symbol of something within. Only a very few have ever heard of this mountain; for the others FitzRoy can be anything, anywhere in the world. What you can do on your own scale for your own soul is all that matters. I don't have to do things that other people may consider difficult anymore. To climb a mountain to see if I can keep from falling off is no reason. To climb a mountain to celebrate my limbs, the sky, my friends, seems better. No, I won't be laying my life on the line for a while. I'll be watching the geese and sniffing the flowers in the meadows.

November 21

Around the governor at his heavy table sit a battalion of rescuers and newsmen. It is their hour now and they have done a good job. I am alone, listening to Spanish being spoken in congratulatory tones, unable to follow the proceedings. It has cost these people barrels of fuel, airplanes from Rio Gallegos, airplanes from B.A., helicopters and men. Three times they had to fly the helicopter up the glacier in heavy gales until at last they were able to haul out Steve's body. Thousands of dollars were spent because our spirits liked to roam, because some kids decided to grow up and know themselves, because some rocks fell from the top of the mountain. Since this whole operation is because of me, I feel I should say something. I thumb through my pocket dictionary and look up the words for "risk" and "gratitude." I thank everyone assembled for spending their money, for making our problem their own, for being such good people. It makes them happy. I am a scraggly vagabond, but also, to these people, a chunk of the United States here in Patagonia. All they ask is that I think well of the Argentine government. I surely do. We all stand up and clap each other on the back. Still no one seems to think it extraordinary or senseless. I meet the two pilots who hauled the body from the crevasse. Around their necks, like medallions from Perón, they wear silver climbing nuts on atrocious pink nylon. On each one is printed "Freakers' Ball 1973."

November 22

The Buenos Aires airport swarms with newsmen in the sweltering heat. Cameras whir and click as the coffin leaves the plane. Adventure and tragedy mean sensation and subscriptions. "Please tell our audience how the deaths occurred," they say over and over again. They are gone because they dared to reach. My admiration is forever for the mountain goat that leaps among the precipices rather than for the domesticated variety complacently grazing. "You say they were only twenty years old. They died so young." You sir, have accumulated more than fifty, but we are all little more than children. I show my tongue to national television, and flash a peace sign from the hearse.

November 24

Homeward bound. This armchair in a padded tube will drop me into another culture with no dust in my eyes. I have lost my best friend. Last week a bag with all my photos, money, and trinkets was stolen. The only souvenir is myself. Across the aisle a physician from Indiana baits me about climbers, death wishes, and homosexuality. His pretentiousness offends me. With reason and rationale he challenges me and makes me think. "Why," he asks. He will not settle for easy answers. I try to tell him.

There is a pleasure and a sense of companionship with the universe that can be found in the elements of stone and ice, flowing things and growing things, blue sky and biting wind. The commitment of the mountaineer is to pursue wholeheartedly to know whole-soulfully the man-shaped essence that he is. I wish to fulfill myself in dance, not in words. Walking skillfully along the top of the world we may receive a priceless vista of our lives and see that which is truly important to us. We may never be able to make sense of why this is so, and if our discoveries are great they always seem to defy words. Still, we may try to elevate the world by sharing our experiences, for the taking and giving are an essential equilibrium that comes from within.

"But you still have not told me of your vision. Surely some words will describe this thing that drives men to do these things, lose their lives. How will you share this elusive treasure?"

I cannot give you the experience, my friend, only the story, the smile, the tear, and if you permit me, the love.

Of all that was Steven, that which is precious is the love that passed between us. Through all the times and troubles, we never lost sight of it.

AN ASCENT OF LONGS PEAK (1879)

Isabella Lucy Bird

Long's Peak, 14,700 feet high, blocks up one end of Estes Park and dwarfs all the surrounding mountains. From it on this side rise, snow-born, the bright St. Vrain and the Big and Little Thompson. By sunlight or moonlight its splintered gray crest is the one object which, in spite of wapiti and bighorn, skunk and grizzly, unfailingly arrests the eye. From it come all storms of snow and wind, and the forked lightning plays round its head like a glory. It is one of the noblest of mountains, but in one's imagination it grows to be much more than a mountain. It becomes invested with a personality. In its caverns and abysses one comes to fancy that it generates and chains the strong winds, to let them loose in its fury. The thunder becomes its voice, and the lightning does it homage. Other summits blush under the morning kiss of the sun, and turn pale the next moment; but it detains the first sunlight and holds it round its head for an hour at least, till it pleases to change from rosy red to deep blue; and the sunset, as if spellbound, lingers latest on its crest. The soft winds which hardly rustle the pine needles down here are raging rudely up there round its motionless summit. The mark of fire is upon it; and though it has passed into a grim repose, it tells of fire and upheaval as truly, though not as eloquently, as the living volcanoes of Hawaii. Here under its shadow one learns how naturally nature worship, and the propitiation of the forces of nature, arose in minds which had no better light.

Long's Peak, "the American Matterhorn," as some call it, was ascended five years ago for the first time. I thought I should like to attempt it, but up to Monday, when Evans left for Denver, cold water was thrown upon the project. It was too late in the season, the winds were likely to be strong, etc.; but just before leaving, Evans said that the weather was looking more settled, and if I did not get farther than the timber-line it would be worth going. Soon after he left, "Mountain Jim" came in and said he would go up as guide, and the two youths who rode here with me from Longmont and I caught at the proposal. Mrs. Edwards at once baked bread for three days, steaks were cut from the steer which hangs up conveniently, and tea, sugar, and butter were benevolently added. Our picnic was not to be a luxurious or "well-found" one, for, in order to avoid the expense of a pack mule, we limited our luggage to what our saddle horses could carry. Behind my saddle I carried three pair of camping blankets and a quilt, which reached to my shoulders. My own boots were so much worn that it was painful to walk, even about the park, in them, so Evans had lent me a pair of his hunting boots, which hung to the horn of my saddle. The horses of the two young men were equally loaded, for we had to prepare for many degrees of frost. Jim was a shocking figure; he had on an old pair of high boots, with a baggy pair of old trousers made of deer hide, held on by an old scarf tucked into them; a leather shirt, with three or four ragged unbuttoned waistcoats over it; an old smashed wideawake, from under which his tawny,

Longs Peak from the east

neglected ringlets hung; and with his one eye, his one long spur, his knife in his belt, his revolver in his waistcoat pocket, his saddle covered with an old beaver skin, from which the paws hung down; his camping blankets behind him, his rifle laid across the saddle in front of him, and his ax, canteen, and other gear hanging to the horn, he was as awful-looking a ruffian as one could see. By way of contrast he rode a small Arab mare of exquisite beauty, skittish, high-spirited, gentle, but altogether too light for him, and he fretted her incessantly to make her display herself.

Heavily loaded as all our horses were, Jim started over the half mile of level grass at a hard gallop, and then throwing his mare on her haunches, pulled up alongside of me, and with a grace of manner which soon made me forget his appearance, entered into a conversation which lasted for more than three hours, in spite of the manifold checks of fording streams single file, abrupt ascents and descents, and other incidents of mountain travel. The ride was one series of glories and surprises, of "park" and glade, of lake and stream, of mountains on mountains, culminating in the rent pinnacles of Long's Peak, which looked yet grander and ghastlier as we crossed an attendant mountain eleven thousand feet high. The slanting sun added fresh beauty every hour. There were dark pines against a lemon sky, gray peaks reddening and etherealizing, gorges of deep and infinite blue, floods of golden glory pouring through canyons of enormous depth, an atmosphere of absolute purity, an occasional foreground of cottonwood and aspen flaunting in red and gold to intensify the blue gloom of the pines, the trickle and murmur of streams fringed with icicles, the strange sough of gusts moving among the pine tops—sights and sounds not of the lower earth, but of the solitary, beast-haunted, frozen upper altitudes. From the dry, buff grass of Estes Park we turned off up a trail on the side of a pine-hung gorge, up a steep pine-clothed hill, down to a small valley, rich in fine, sun-cured hay about eighteen inches high, and enclosed by high mountains whose deepest hollow contains a lily-covered lake, fitly named "the Lake of the Lilies." Ah, how magical its beauty was as it slept in silence, while there the dark pines were mirrored motionless in its pale gold, and here the great white lily cups and dark green leaves rested on amethyst-colored water!

From this we ascended into the purple gloom of great pine forests which clothe the skirts of the mountains up to a height of about eleven thousand feet, and from their chill and solitary depths we had glimpses of golden atmosphere and rose-lit summits, not of "the land very far off" but of the land nearer now in all its grandeur, gaining in sublimity by nearness—glimpses, too, through a broken vista of purple gorges, of the illimitable Plains lying idealized in the late sunlight, their baked, brown expanse transfigured into the likeness of a sunset sea rolling infinitely in waves of misty gold.

We rode upwards through the gloom on a steep trail blazed through the forest, all my intellect concentrated on avoiding being dragged off my horse by impending branches or having the blankets badly torn, as those of my companions were, by sharp dead limbs, between which there was hardly room to pass—the horses breathless and requiring to stop every few yards, though their riders, except myself, were afoot. The gloom of the dense, ancient, silent forest is to me awe inspiring. On such an evening it is soundless, except for the branches creaking in the soft wind, the frequent snap of decayed timber, and a murmur in the pine tops as of a not-distant waterfall, all tending to produce eeriness and a sadness "hardly akin to pain." There no lumberer's ax has ever rung. The trees die when they have attained their prime, and stand there, dead and bare, till the fierce mountain winds lay them prostrate. The pines grew smaller and more sparse as we ascended, and the last stragglers wore a tortured, warring look. The timberline was passed, but yet a little higher a slope of mountain meadow dipped to the southwest toward a bright stream trickling under ice and icicles, and there a grove of the beautiful silver spruce marked our camping ground. The trees were in miniature, but so exquisitely arranged that one might well ask what artist's hand had planted them, scattering them here, clumping them there, and training their slim spires toward heaven. Hereafter, when I call up memories of the glorious, the view from this camping ground will come up.

Looking east, gorges opened to the distant Plains, then fading into purple-gray. Mountains with pine-clothed skirts rose in ranges, or, solitary, uplifted their gray summits, while close behind, but nearly three thousand feet above us, towered the bald white crest of Long's Peak, its huge precipices red with the light of a sun long lost to our eyes. Close to us, in the caverned side of the peak, was snow that, owing to its position, is eternal. Soon the afterglow came on, and before it faded a big half-moon hung out of the heavens, shining through the silver-blue foliage of the pines on the frigid background of snow, and turning the whole into fairyland.

A courageous Denver artist attempted the ascent just before I arrived but, after camping out at the timberline for a week, was foiled by the perpetual storms and was driven down again, leaving some very valuable apparatus about three thousand feet from the summit.

Unsaddling and picketing the horses securely, making the beds of pine shoots, and dragging up logs for fuel warmed us all. Jim built up a great fire, and before long we were all sitting around it at supper. It didn't matter much that we had to drink our tea out of the battered meat tins in which it was boiled, and eat strips of beef reeking with pine smoke without plates or forks.

"Treat Jim as a gentleman and you'll find him one," I had been told; and though his manner was certainly bolder and freer than that of gentlemen generally, no imaginary fault could be found. He was very agreeable as a man of culture as well as a child of nature; the desperado was altogether out of sight. He was very courteous and even kind to me, which was fortunate, as the young men had little idea of showing even ordinary civilities. That night I made the acquaintance of his dog, "Ring," said to be the best hunting dog in Colorado, with the body and legs of a collie but a head approaching that of a mastiff, a noble face with a wistful human expression and the most truthful eyes I ever saw in an animal. His master loves him if he loves anything, but in his savage moods ill-treats him. Ring's devotion never swerves, and his truthful eyes are rarely taken off his master's face. He is almost human in his intelligence, and, unless he is told to do so, he never takes notice of anyone but Jim. In a tone as if speaking to a human being, his master, pointing to me, said, "Ring, go to that lady, and don't leave her again tonight." Ring at once came to me, looked into my face, laid his head on my shoulder, and then lay down beside me with his head on my lap but never taking his eyes from Jim's face.

The long shadows of the pines lay upon the frosted grass, an aurora leaped fitfully, and the moonlight, though intensely bright, was pale beside the red, leaping flames of our pine logs and their red glow on our gear, ourselves, and Ring's truthful face. One of the young men sang a Latin student's song and two Negro melodies; the other, "Sweet Spirit, Hear my Prayer." Jim sang one of Moore's melodies in a singular falsetto, and all together sang "The Star Spangled Banner" and "The Red, White, and Blue." Then Jim recited a very clever poem of his own composition and told some fearful Indian stories. A group of small silver spruces away from the fire was my sleeping place. The artist who had been up there had so woven and interlaced their lower branches as to form a bower, affording at once shelter from the wind and a most agreeable privacy. It was thickly strewn with young pine shoots, and these, when covered with a blanket, with an inverted saddle for a pillow, made a luxurious bed. The mercury at 9:00 p.m. was twelve degrees below the freezing point. Jim, after a last look at the horses, made a huge fire, and stretched himself out beside it, but Ring lay at my back to keep me warm. I could not sleep, but the night passed rapidly. I was anxious about the ascent, for gusts of ominous sound swept through the pines at intervals. Then wild animals howled, and Ring was perturbed in spirit about them. Then it was strange to see the notorious desperado, a red-handed man, sleeping as quietly as innocence sleeps. But, above all, it was exciting to lie there, with no better shelter than a bower of pines, on a mountain eleven thousand feet high, in the very heart of the Rocky Range, under twelve degrees of frost, hearing sounds of wolves, with shivering stars looking through the fragrant canopy, with arrowy pines for bedposts, and for a night lamp the red flames of a campfire.

Day dawned long before the sun rose, pure and lemon colored. The rest were looking after the horses, when one of the students came running to tell me that I must come farther down the slope, for Jim said he had never seen such a sunrise. From the chill, gray peak above, from the everlasting snows, from the silvered pines, down through mountain ranges with their depths of Tyrian purple, we looked to where the Plains lay cold, in blue-gray, like a morning sea against a far horizon. Suddenly, as a dazzling streak at first, but enlarging rapidly into a dazzling sphere, the sun wheeled above the gray line, as light and glorious as when it was first created. Jim involuntarily and reverently uncovered his head, and exclaimed, "I believe there is a God!" I felt as if,

Parsee-like, I must worship. The gray of the Plains changed to purple, the sky was all one rose-red flush on which vermilion cloud-streaks rested; the ghastly peaks gleamed like rubies, the earth and heavens were newly created. Surely "the Most High dwelleth not in temples made with hands!" For a full hour those Plains simulated the ocean, down to whose limitless expanse of purple, cliffs, rocks, and promontories swept down.

By seven we had finished breakfast and passed into the ghastlier solitudes above, I riding as far as what, rightly or wrongly, are called the "Lava Beds," an expanse of large and small boulders, with snow in their crevices. It was very cold; some water which we crossed was frozen hard enough to bear the horses. Jim had advised me against taking any wraps, and my thin Hawaiian riding dress, only fit for the tropics, was penetrated by the keen air. The rarefied atmosphere soon began to oppress our breathing, and I found that Evans's boots were so large that I had no foothold. Fortunately, before the real difficulty of the ascent began, we found, under a rock, a pair of small overshoes, probably left by the Hayden exploring expedition, which just lasted for the day. As we were leaping from rock to rock, Jim said, "I was thinking in the night about your travelling alone, and wondering where you carried your Derringer, for I could see no signs of it." On my telling him that I traveled unarmed, he could hardly believe it, and adjured me to get a revolver at once.

On arriving at the "Notch" (a literal gate of rock), we found ourselves absolutely on the knifelike ridge or backbone of Long's Peak, only a few feet wide, covered with colossal boulders and fragments, and on the other side shelving in one precipitous, snow-patched sweep of three thousand feet to a picturesque hollow, containing a lake of pure green water. Other lakes, hidden among dense pine woods, were farther off, while close above us rose the peak, which, for about five hundred feet, is a smooth, gaunt, inaccessible-looking pile of granite. Passing through the Notch, we looked along the nearly inaccessible side of the peak, composed of boulders and debris of all shapes and sizes, through which appeared broad, smooth ribs of reddish-colored granite, looking as if they upheld the towering rock mass above.

I usually dislike bird's-eye and panoramic views, but, though from a mountain, this was not one. Serrated ridges, not much lower than that on which we stood, rose, one beyond another, as far as that pure atmosphere could carry the vision, broken into awful chasms deep with ice and snow, rising into pinnacles piercing the heavenly blue with their cold, barren gray, on, on forever, till the most distant range upbore unsullied snow alone. There were fair lakes mirroring the dark pine woods, canyons dark and blue-black with unbroken expanses of pines, snow-slashed pinnacles, wintry heights frowning upon lovely parks, watered and wooded, lying in the lap of summer; North Park floating off into the blue distance, Middle Park closed till another season, the sunny slopes of Estes Park, and winding down among the mountains the snowy ridge of the Divide, whose bright waters seek both the Atlantic and Pacific Oceans. There, far below, links of diamonds showed where the Grand River takes its rise to seek the mysterious Colorado, with its still unsolved enigma, and loses itself in the waters of the Pacific; and nearer the snow-born Thompson bursts forth from the ice to begin its journey to the Gulf of Mexico.

Nature, rioting in her grandest mood, exclaimed with voices of grandeur, solitude, sublimity, beauty, and infinity, "Lord, what is man, that Thou art mindful of him? or the son of man, that Thou visitest him?" Never-to-be-forgotten glories they were, burnt in upon my memory by six succeeding hours of terror.

You know I have no head and no ankles, and never ought to dream of mountaineering; and had I known that the ascent was a real mountaineering feat I should not have felt the slightest ambition to perform it. As it is, I am only humiliated by my success, for Jim dragged me up, like a bale of goods, by sheer force of muscle. At the Notch the real business of the ascent began. Two thousand feet of solid rock towered above us, four thousand feet of broken rock shelved precipitously below; smooth granite ribs, with barely a foothold, stood out here and there; melted snow, refrozen several times, presented a more serious obstacle; many of the rocks were loose, and tumbled down when touched. To me it was a time of extreme terror. I was roped to Jim, but it was of no use; my feet were paralyzed and slipped on the bare rock, and he said it was useless to try to go that way, and we retraced our steps.

I wanted to return to the Notch, knowing that my incompetence would detain the party, and one of the young men said almost plainly that a woman was a dangerous encumbrance, but the trapper replied shortly that if it were not to take a lady up he would not go up at all. He went on to explore, and reported that further progress on the correct line of ascent was blocked by ice; and then for two hours we descended, lowering ourselves by our hands from rock to rock along a boulder-strewn sweep of four thousand feet, patched with ice and snow, and perilous from rolling stones. My fatigue, giddiness, and pain from bruised ankles, and arms half pulled out of their sockets, were so great that I should never have gone halfway had not Jim, *nolens volens*, dragged me along with a patience and skill, and withal a determination that I should ascend the peak, which never failed. After descending about two thousand feet to avoid the ice, we got into a deep ravine with inaccessible sides, partly filled with ice and snow and partly with large and small fragments of rock, which were constantly giving way, rendering the footing very insecure. That part to me was two hours of painful and unwilling submission to the inevitable; of trembling, slipping, straining, of smooth ice appearing when it was least expected, and of weak entreaties to be left behind while the others went on. Jim always said that there was no danger, that there was only a short bad bit ahead, and that I should go up even if he carried me!

Slipping, faltering, gasping from the exhausting toil in the rarefied air, with throbbing hearts and panting lungs, we reached the top of the gorge and squeezed ourselves between two gigantic fragments of rock by a passage called the "Dog's Lift," when I climbed on the shoulders of one man and then was hauled up. This introduced us by an abrupt turn round the southwest angle of the peak to a narrow shelf of considerable length, rugged, uneven, and so overhung by the cliff in some places that it is necessary to crouch to pass at all. Above, the peak looks nearly vertical for four hundred feet; and below, the most tremendous precipice I have ever seen descends in one unbroken fall. This is usually considered the most dangerous part of the ascent, but it does not seem so to me, for such foothold as is there is secure, and one fancies that it is possible to hold on with the hands. But there, and on the final, and, to my thinking, the worst part of the climb, one slip, and a breathing, thinking, human being would lie three thousand feet below, a shapeless, bloody heap! Ring refused to traverse the "Ledge" and remained at the "Lift," howling piteously.

Thence the view is more magnificent even than that from the Notch. At the foot of the precipice below us lay a lovely lake, wood embosomed, from or near which the bright St. Vrain and other streams take their rise. I thought how their clear cold waters, growing turbid in the affluent flats, would heat under the tropic sun and eventually form part of that great ocean river which renders our far-off islands habitable by impinging on their shores. Snowy ranges, one behind the other, extended to the distant horizon, folding in their wintry embrace the beauties of Middle Park. Pike's Peak, more than one hundred miles off, lifted that vast but shapeless summit which is the landmark of southern Colorado. There were snow patches, snow slashes, snow abysses, snow forlorn and soiled looking, snow pure and dazzling, snow glistening above the purple robe of pine worn by all the mountains; while away to the east, in limitless breadth, stretched the green-gray of the endless Plains. Giants everywhere reared their splintered crests. Thence, with a single sweep, the eye takes in a distance of three hundred miles—that distance to the west, north, and south being made up of mountains ten, eleven, twelve, and thirteen thousand feet in height, dominated by Long's Peak, Gray's Peak, and Pike's Peak, all nearly the height of Mont Blanc! On the Plains we traced the rivers by their fringe of cottonwoods to the distant Platte, and between us and them lay glories of mountain, canyon, and lake, sleeping in depths of blue and purple most ravishing to the eye.

As we crept from the ledge round a horn of rock, I beheld what made me perfectly sick and dizzy to look at—the terminal peak itself—a smooth, cracked face or wall of pink granite, as nearly perpendicular as anything could well be up which it was possible to climb, well deserving the name of the "American Matterhorn."

Scaling, not climbing, is the correct term for this last ascent. It took one hour to accomplish five hundred feet, pausing for breath every minute or two. The only foothold was in narrow cracks or on minute projections on the granite. To get a toe in these cracks, or here and there on a scarcely obvious projection, while crawling on hands and knees, all the while tortured with thirst and gasping and struggling for breath, this was the climb; but at last the peak was won. A grand, well-defined mountaintop it is, a nearly level acre of boulders, with precipitous sides all round, the one we came up being the only accessible one.

It was not possible to remain long. One of the young men was seriously alarmed by bleeding from the lungs, and the intense dryness of the day and the rarefaction of the air, at a height of nearly fifteen thousand feet, made respiration very painful. There is always water on the peak, but it was frozen as hard as a rock, and the sucking of ice and snow increases thirst. We all suffered severely from the want of water, and the gasping for breath made our mouths and tongues so dry that articulation was difficult and the speech of all unnatural.

From the summit were seen in unrivalled combination all the views which had rejoiced our eyes during the ascent. It was something at last to stand upon the storm-rent crown of this lonely sentinel of the Rocky Range, on one of the mightiest of the vertebrae of the backbone of the North

American continent, and to see the waters start for both oceans. Uplifted above love and hate and storms of passion, calm amidst the eternal silences, fanned by zephyrs and bathed in living blue, peace rested for that one bright day on the peak, as if it were some region

> *Where falls not rain, or hail, or any snow,*
> *Or ever wind blows loudly.*

We placed our names, with the date of ascent, in a tin within a crevice, and descended to the Ledge, sitting on the smooth granite, getting our feet into cracks and against projections, and letting ourselves down by our hands, Jim going before me so that I might steady my feet against his powerful shoulders. I was no longer giddy, and faced the precipice of thirty-five hundred feet without a shiver. Repassing the Ledge and Lift, we accomplished the descent through fifteen hundred feet of ice and snow, with many falls and bruises, but no worse mishap, and there separated, the young men taking the steepest but most direct way to the Notch, with the intention of getting ready for the march home; and Jim and I taking what he thought the safer route for me—a descent over boulders for two thousand feet, and then a tremendous ascent to the Notch. I had various falls, and once hung by my frock, which caught on a rock, and Jim severed it with his hunting knife, upon which I fell into a crevice full of soft snow. We were driven lower down the mountains than he had intended by impassable tracts of ice, and the ascent was tremendous. For the last two hundred feet the boulders were of enormous size, and the steepness fearful. Sometimes I drew myself up on hands and knees, sometimes crawled;

I would not now exchange my memories of its perfect beauty and extraordinary sublimity for any other experience of mountaineering in any part of the world. Yesterday snow fell on the summit, and it will be inaccessible for eight months to come.

Let no practical mountaineer be allured by my description into the ascent of Long's Peak. Truly terrible as it was to me, to a member of the Alpine Club it would not be a feat worth performing.

THE GREAT AND SECRET SHOW (1997)

Warren Hollinger

Clive Barker's novel *The Great and Secret Show* asserts there is a hallowed place of intense existence so pure and euphoric it can only be reached three times in your life: at birth, the first moments you truly experience love, and at death. Once attained, the profound memory lingers in our subconscious, but we can only endure until our demise before we are one last time graced by its presence. For every climber there exists one experience that stands out as the most intensely absorbed moment of his or her life—a moment so sharp that the rest of the world blurs into trivial extinction. Though the climber may try over and over to duplicate the formula, he never quite manages to revisit this lost ground.

In 1995, Mark Synnott and I, with Jerry Gore, traveled to Baffin Island's northeastern fjords and climbed the Great Cross Pillar, letting the monolith of the Polar Sun Spire stare us down for the thirteen days of our ascent. We realized that wall had captured a piece of our soul, and we needed to retrieve it. Though none of us could truly conceive of the depths we would have to dig to pull off such an ascent, nor even understand our own motives for enduring a stay on a wall three times longer than any of us had previously experienced, our belief in the mission was unshakable. In the frigid days of May 1996, Mark, Jeff Chapman, and I approached the Polar Sun Spire another time. For three men ready to step foot on the north face, the show was about to begin.

May 21, 1996

I have absolutely no idea what day it is today, or even whether it is morning or evening. But that's how it is out here. We work day and night to establish a position from which we can mount an all-out effort on this face. Twenty-four-hour light affords us strategies rarely contemplated in a more southern latitude. Climbing sessions of twenty to thirty hours become the norm; our clocks now run on a thirty-six-hour day. After three days of fixing and one thousand feet of rope, all that is left is to rise into the abyss and search out our own meaning to this adventure. And become lost in the show.

June 8, 1996 (Day: 15; On Wall: 12; Last Push: 3)

First hanging bivy above the snow ledge. We have five haul bags, three bullet bags, one bucket, two portaledges, and the ability, we believe, to stay on the wall for thirty days. We're sixteen hundred feet up the route, six hundred feet above the ledge, and just beginning the arduous task of navigating a way through the two-thousand-foot overhanging sea of seams and ripples.

Two men work to advance our position, while the other whiles away his day reading and ignoring the roar of his stomach. We've spent twelve nights on the wall. Went down for more food and fuel on June 4 after eighteen gallons of water froze solid and we determined that three and a half gallons of fuel was not enough. A radio call was made; family and friends were informed that the wall required four more weeks of climbing, our airline tickets needed to be changed, and the

Warren Hollinger

odds of being stranded during ice breakup were high. Once resupplied, we spent twenty-six hours repacking our gear and headed back up the wall June 6 . . .

The wall is completely overhanging for the last six hundred feet. No way to get into the anchors. We are totally committed now. There is a relief in the finality, and our new concern is focused upon our water supply. The next ledge is a steep and intricate thirteen hundred feet away.

June 12, 1996 (Day: 19; On Wall: 15; Last Push: 7)
We're all a bit edgy and probably have one lightly heated argument every day or two. Everything gets resolved and we always go back to our usual routine. Generally food (lack of food, that is) seems to be the source of our disagreements. . . . We've upped our rations to have more snacking food. I hope this is a good strategy.

It sounds like a war zone around here: Missiles fly by, crashing into ledges below us. It's pretty wild, but it's becoming routine . . .

Today has turned out quite nice It's Mark's lead and I have a day off. I cleaned up the rock dust and shrapnel chunks out of the ledge, straightened things up a bit and repaired a burn hole in Jeff's sleeping bag. (He's been smoking three to five cigarettes a day. He's definitely not a practiced smoker.) We've been working well as a team like that, drying out each other's bags, repairing each other's shit . . .

I sometimes secretly wish we could stay up here longer. On the mellow days there seems to be no other place in the world I would rather be. The living is hard but comfortable. The quiet is so fantastic—not another human being for eighty miles. No sound except the air in your ears (and those rock missiles).

People think we're crazy, but they have no idea the world they are missing . . .

We're moving like slugs, but still trying to remember to enjoy the process, not the goal.

June 17, 1996 (Day: 24; On Wall: 21; Last Push: 11)

It's my day off again. It's also the day we were to be picked up and brought to Clyde River. That is definitely not to be! We are twenty-six hundred feet up the wall and have no intentions of returning until we reach the top.

We moved our bivy a couple of shifts ago. After Mark's fourteen-hour pitch (a real scrappy one), Jeff led for ten hours. It snowed on me for six hours, a wet one, almost rain (we've been hoping it doesn't rain, that would really screw us up), that kept me huddled in my belay bag, wishing I were somewhere else.

The wall has been wearing on us. I heard Mark say the other day, "It feels like we've been on this wall for a year." Twenty-four days, actually, but who's counting? Most days I actually forget what day of the week it is, what time it is, or how long we've been on the wall. And I never know the day of the week . . .

The actual climbing on this route is proving similar to the sunny Yosemite walls we trained on, but the adventure is a whole world apart. The placements, though familiar in technique and difficulty, always appear more awkward on a first ascent in double boots, gloves, and four layers of clothing. Though we have all done hard aid in these conditions, thirteen-hour leads become common ground. Serious A2 could take eight to ten hours and the face never eases off during the overhanging two-thousand-foot section. The steepness combined with the incipient nature of this part of the wall has everyone digging for their absolute mental, physical, and emotional best.

Actually, it's easy to find your best when the consequences for anything less are, well, unthinkable.

At the end of Jeff's pitch the angle finally kicks back to vertical. After ten long pitches of overhanging climbing with the shortest pitches taking nine or ten hours, we are happy to see continuous cracks and vertical to less-than-vertical climbing. With one gallon of water to spare, we hit our first snow ledge. Three quarts per person per day for twelve days has just sufficed. With snow every few hundred feet, water will never again be a concern. Now, if only the food, fuel, and weather would hold.

June 22, 1996 (Day: 29; On Wall: 26; Last Push: 16)

It's a bit unnerving listening to the avalanches hitting all around the ledge every thirty to sixty seconds. I hear the missiles coming and for an eternity I can't decide whether it will be a direct hit or a near miss. The sun wreaks havoc up here. It stormed for the last five days and my altimeter dropped five hundred feet yesterday, signifying high pressure and a good spell of weather. Great for climbing, bad for the bivy. The guys headed out at 5:00 p.m. on Pitch 22; by 10:00 p.m. the sun hit us, and by 12:00 a.m. the bigger slides started sloughing off.

Our bivy is on the middle snow ledge above the overhangs. We reached this ledge about three days ago (hard to think in days—two pushes ago). It's the psychological turning point for the team. With the most demanding part (technically and mentally) behind us, summiting is inevitable. The only question now is when. I approximate the height on the wall right now to be around three thousand feet . . .

. . . I look out at a view I will never experience again, and am dumbfounded by its beauty. There will be other walls *in the future, yet this one is now and its majestic panorama is like no other in the world. The frozen ocean, cracked in a couple of dozen places for miles across the fjord, splits twenty two-thousand-foot-plus walls. The snow has almost entirely left the ice. The reflections and shadows are staggering.*

As to the tidbits around camp: My toes are fuzzy feeling, and sometimes numb, yet they are functioning fine. My double boot welt is trashed; no crampon will ever see this boot again. I've been sewing up a storm, trying to add some extra life to our glove liners. Hoping a large pile of snow doesn't blow through the portaledge while I'm writing this down. Basically having a great time! I know one day this will all be over and I'll long to be back up here again, so I'm definitely going to make the most of it.

Upper snow is now melting away, granting passage on bare, featured rock. Our only real concern at this point is the sea ice: Will it stay long enough to get us home—or is it perhaps already too late?

June 28, 1996 (Day: 35; On Wall: 32; Last Push: 22)

We're all feeling pretty good right now. Spent, but good. From Camp V, six hundred feet above the snow ledge, we made a twenty-four-hour push and set the anchors for Camp VI, six hundred feet at the top of the pillar. We established this camp (Camp V) four days ago with a 5.9 A1 loose lead by me and Mark with a scrappy ice chimney that he was able to get into the back of and ice climb (WI3), which gave us a water ice rating. He brought us to a ledge that is the most incredible perch I've ever seen. The view is phenomenal. The portaledge sits at the edge of the pillar thirty-five hundred feet up the route. We're over the Great Cross Pillar. Substantially!

It really gives us a sense that this is almost over when we start seeing everything from this height. Being almost over is a relief. It's been a long time up to here. We really would like to finish this climb and get on with our lives. At least, I know I would.

Since we got what we thought might take three days done in one push, we celebrated by getting an extra piece of cheese and an extra can of tuna in our combined dinner pot. Doesn't sound like much, but it is unfortunately splurging for us. We'll haul today sometime, but we need to get some sleep now. I've been asleep for only six hours, but I woke up with my stomach growling. It's feeding time, and I don't get fed. My body screams for more nourishment, but all it gets is scraps, and then only at the appointed times. I'll figure out a way to sleep—or I won't sleep at all. Them's the breaks.

We think we can traverse a snow ledge from Camp VI to the ridge and summit on our next push. That would be fantastic. I hope we find the climbing easy and get there in just a few hours, but there looks to be some steep rock on the top of the ridge. The picture shows tons of snow along the way, but I think (I hope) we'll have mostly dry rock. If this window of weather holds for a couple more days, we may get a perfectly clear summit. Then it's rapping the wall and back to base camp to call the outfitters and let everyone know we're okay.

Whew, it's almost over. Unless of course we can't get back because of the ocean ice conditions. Then it will be another four to six weeks. Shit! I guess we'll go climbing (that's if the outfitter left us the extra food). We'll see. Well, I'm going to try to sleep. Big day of hauling today. Maybe that will shut my stomach up.

To find a set of inobvious features from the ground, believing they will ultimately create a passage that will keep you alive and carry you to the top, has always appeared to me as one of the great challenges of rock climbing. When the plan unfolds and the pieces of the puzzle fall into perfect place, you recognize at that moment that you are truly at one with your environment. Speak not of conquering, for those who believe they can impose their will on such a shrine to nature will be sadly mistaken—if they are lucky enough to escape alive.

I recognize in hindsight there was much more to our success than tenacity and know-how. To live on a wall for so long teaches you an unsurpassed respect for the omnipotence of your environment and a realization that if it's your time to go, any one of a thousand things can readily take you there. Our goal, therefore, as in all the disciplines of climbing, was not to focus on what could go wrong, but just on the next move. And after that, the next. The scope of the project was much too large for our puny minds to grasp in one sitting.

And so on July 1, 1996, twenty-five days after leaving the ground for the final time, we found ourselves embraced in a group hug on the top of our dream. The feeling was not necessarily elation: We all knew somehow deep within that we would ultimately make it. No, it was more like relief, happiness, sadness. Finality. That's it: Finality. We had lost ourselves in this adventure as if in a riveting book that couldn't be put down, and now that the show was complete, the last page turned, we realized we could never again revisit this ground. No matter how hard we might try, "The Great and Secret Show" would be no more.

MOUNT ASSINIBOINE (1905)

James Outram

Three chief causes have combined to bring Mount Assiniboine into special prominence among the peaks of Canada. First, its remarkable resemblance from certain aspects to the world-famed Matterhorn; though perhaps the Dent Blanche is more nearly its prototype in the better-known Swiss Alps. Secondly, the exquisite photographs and fascinating descriptions of Mr. W. D. Wilcox, the principal explorer of that region and the mountain's earliest biographer. And, lastly, the fact that it has repelled more assaults by mountain climbers than any other peak in the Canadian Rockies, and gained a reputation at one time of extreme difficulty or even inaccessibility.

Its massive pyramid forms a conspicuous landmark from almost every considerable eminence for scores of miles around, towering fully fifteen hundred feet above its neighbours, and by its isolation no less than by its splendid outline commanding attention and admiration.

It enjoys the proud distinction of being the loftiest mountain south of the railroad, 11,860 feet above sea level, and is situated on the continental watershed; and its mighty mass, with five huge spurs, covers an area of some thirty square miles and harbours fully a dozen picturesque lakes within the shelter of its giant arms.

The peak is grandest from its northern side. It rises, like a monster tooth, from an entourage of dark cliff and gleaming glacier, five thousand feet above the valley of approach; the magnificent triangular face, barred with horizontal belts of perpendicular cliff and glistening expanses of the purest snow and ice, which constitutes the chief glory of the mountain, soaring more than three thousand feet directly from the glacier that sweeps its base. On the eastern and the southern sides the walls and buttresses are practically sheer precipices five to six thousand feet in vertical height, but the contour and character of the grand northern face more than compensate for the less sheer and lofty precipices.

The mighty monolith was named in 1885 by Dr. G. M. Dawson, of the Dominion Geological Survey, from a tribe of Indians inhabiting the plains, but he and his party only viewed it from afar. The first white men to explore the immediate vicinity, so far as can be learned, were Messrs. R. L. Barrett and T. E. Wilson, who, in 1893, made an expedition to the mountain's base. The latter is a famous pioneer of the Canadian Rockies, with probably a greater knowledge of them than any man has ever yet possessed, and his store of yarns, drawn almost entirely from personal experience or that of his immediate associates, is as full of interest and valuable information as it is extensive. He and Mr. Barrett crossed the Simpson Pass and followed down the Simpson River to the mouth of a tributary flowing straight from the direction of Mount Assiniboine. Ascending this with infinite difficulty, they crossed over to the North Fork of the Cross River and thence upward to their goal.

The ensuing summer Mr. S. E. S. Allen visited the northern side by the same route, and the next year both Mr. Allen and Mr. Barrett again succumbed to the fascinations of the neighbourhood and were found once more encamped under the shadow of the monarch of the southern Rockies. The latter traveller was accompanied by Mr. J. F. Porter and Mr. W. D. Wilcox, who made some careful observations for altitude, and has given us a charming and instructive description of his wanderings in his magnificently illustrated book, *The Rockies of Canada*. Messrs. Barrett and Wilcox with Bill Peyto completed the circuit of the mountain on foot, a laborious but interesting undertaking which occupied them a fraction more than two days. Beautiful valleys, heading in glaciers and adorned with lakes, alternated with rough and precipitous intervening ridges, each in turn having to be crossed. A large portion of the first day was spent traversing a valley devastated by a huge forest fire; the denseness of the charred and fallen trunks, sometimes piled ten or twelve feet above the ground, rendered progress painfully slow and toilsome, and, on emerging "'black as coal-heavers from our long walk in the burnt timber, seeking a refuge in the rocky ledges of the mountains, and clad in uncouth garments torn and discolored, we must,' writes Mr. Wilcox, 'have resembled the aboriginal savages of this wild region.'" (*The Rockies of Canada*) Finally, by following a tiny goat track, discovered on the face of a dangerous-looking ridge, they reached the valley of the North Fork of the Cross River, falling in with Messrs. Smith and Allen, encamped in that pleasant spot and bent on similar investigations, and early next morning regained their camp on the shore of Lake Assiniboine.

Amongst the many valuable results of this complete inspection of the massif from every point of the compass, much information appealing particularly to the mountaineer was obtained. The contour of the main peak was shown to be very different from the symmetrical cone anticipated by the view from the north; the previously hidden southern ridge was found to extend a considerable distance at a comparatively easy angle to an abrupt and absolutely vertical precipice, and broken only by a deep notch that transforms the southern extremity into a sharp subsidiary peak. The eastern face defies approach to the summit from that direction, as does the southern buttress, but the southwestern side developed a more practicable line of ascent and one that offered every prospect of success.

Not until 1899, however, was any attempt made to scale these attractive heights. That summer Mr. Wilcox returned to the neighbourhood accompanied by Mr. H. G. Bryant, of Philadelphia, well known to those interested in Arctic exploration, and Mr. L. J. Steele, an Englishman. These two were the first to attack the formidable citadel, and narrowly escaped losing their lives in the attempt. They ascended the northwest arête to an altitude of about ten thousand feet, when they were compelled to desist after several hours of hard climbing, an approaching storm assisting to hasten their descent. "They had just come to the top of the last ice slope, when Steele's foothold gave way, and he fell, dragging Bryant after him. There was but one possible escape from a terrible fall. A projecting rock of considerable size appeared not far below, and Steele, with a skillful lunge of his ice ax, swung round to it and anchored himself in a narrow crevice, where the snow had melted away. No sooner had he come to a stop than Bryant shot over him from above and likewise found safety. Otherwise they would have fallen about six hundred feet, with serious, if not fatal, results." (W. D. Wilcox in *The Rockies of Canada*.)

Another year went by, and a far more serious climbing expedition was fitted out to try to conquer the now famous mountain. Two brothers, the Messrs. Walling, of Chicago, with larger enthusiasm than experience in matters mountaineering, took with them three Swiss guides to force a way to the tantalizing summit. Camping, as usual, by the side of Lake Assiniboine, they followed Steele and Bryant's route to the northern glacier, ascending thence directly toward the apex by rock outcrops and snow slopes. So far so good, though progress was extremely slow even on such an easy task; but when they came to the lowest belt of vertical cliffs the retreat was sounded, and for the second time victory rested with Mount Assiniboine.

On the return to Banff the shortest route (geographically) was taken, by White Man Pass and down the Spray Valley, but through some mismanagement or worse, the guides went on ahead, the Wallings were lost and, so the story goes, reduced to slaying a horse for sustenance before they were discovered by a search party. But the whole proceedings of the climb and the return were never very fully given to the public.

Thus far the northwest arête and the north face had been unsuccessfully approached, but Mr. Wilcox, mindful of the easier appearance of the southwestern side, in 1901 made a determined effort to achieve victory from that direction. Mr. Bryant and two Swiss guides, E. Feuz and F. Michel, completed the party.

The main difficulty of this route was the approach to the mountain's base with a camping outfit, my more recent plan of access never having been deemed worthy of consideration as even entering the region of practicability. So eventually, after a long and toilsome march, they found themselves encamped in the deep gorge beneath the huge steep mass of the great peak. I shall have more to say concerning this side and their line of ascent later; suffice it now briefly to chronicle that, after attaining an altitude of 10,850 feet (just one thousand feet below the top), the avalanching appearance of the snow, the difficulties beyond, the lateness of the hour, and the overburdening of Feuz (Michel having had an accident on the way out) combined to drive them back.

Thus the fortress still remained inviolate; the eastern side a precipice, the southern equally impossible, the northern and southwestern faces, if possibly accessible, yet strongly guarded, each holding a record of an attack repelled. The glaciers had proved too much for the first party of assailants, the solid rampart of the first line of fortifications beat back the next assault, and on the opener, more vulnerable side, alpine artillery had to be brought into play in order to defeat the last attempt. Who should be the next to storm the citadel and what the outcome?

This question was uppermost in many minds when the disappointing news of the last failure became known, and the pros and cons were most exhaustively debated around Mr. Whymper's campfire in the upper Yoho Valley, where I was having a glorious time amongst the untrodden peaks and glaciers of that delightful region. Peyto, our outfitter, Mr. Wilcox's companion on the circuit of Mount Assiniboine six years before, added much fuel to the already consuming desire to examine and if possible ascend the mountain, but the distance and expense placed the enterprise beyond my reach, and I had sadly given up the whole idea when Peyto, asserting that for experienced mountaineers there was absolutely no question of a failure, pledged himself that if I would go and see and conquer he would undertake to get me there within two days from Banff and bring me back in less; and he proved even better than his word, although the journey had never previously been made in less than three days.

At the end of August, therefore, the weather being fine, though showing indications of the inevitable break which comes each year about this date, bringing a snowstorm to usher in the Indian summer of September, the opportunity arrived. It was "now or never" for this season, so I resolved to make a dash for the peak before the snow should render it impossible, and, Peyto being ready, a start upon the 31st was hastily arranged.

Thanks to the ready and able cooperation of Miss Mollison, the incomparable manager of the Hotel at Field, provisions, blankets, etc., were rapidly collected, and on the afternoon of the 30th Christian Häsler, Christian Bohren, and I were in the train bound for Banff. Here we were met by Peyto and conducted to our tent pitched amongst the bushes near the bank of the Bow River. Our object was kept entirely secret, and scarcely a soul knew of the starting of the expedition at all.

The next morning was occupied in final arrangements, making up the packs and loading up, and eventually at half-past one the procession set out. First the cavalry; Bill Peyto, picturesque and workmanlike, led the way upon his trusty mare, then followed four packhorses, the fastest and most reliable of Peyto's bunch, laden with tents, provisions, and our miscellaneous impedimenta; and Jack Sinclair, our assistant packer, also mounted, brought up the rear, to stimulate laggards and maintain the pace. Then came the infantry, comprising the two Christians and myself. Both the guides were tried companions, especially Häsler, who had already made several first ascents with me.

Mount Assiniboine is only distant from Banff twenty miles in an air-line, yet by the shortest route it cannot be reached in twice that length of march; the trails are rough and often blocked with fallen timber, and no small amount of climbing is involved. But all of us were keen and determined each to do his best to make the journey to the base a record and the expedition a success.

The afternoon was sultry, with a haze about the summits and a look toward the west that boded rain; but the barometer stood well and hope was high.

At first we passed along the dusty road, with the cool, peaceful Bow eddying alongside, hemmed in by green banks, with overhanging branches dipping lazily in the current. Then we turned off into a winding trail that meandered among alders and small timber, with fallen logs and an occasional morass to vary the monotony. Close by, an eagle's nest hung in the branches of an isolated tree, the memorial of a domestic tragedy. Earlier in the summer Mr. Whymper had discovered it, had the two fine parent birds shot as specimens, each measuring over six feet from tip to tip of wing, and sent the baby to the aviary at Vancouver.

Behind us rose the impressive walls of Cascade Mountain; on our right, across the valley, the sharp pinnacles of Mount Edith pierced the sky; and wooded slopes flanked us on the left and rose to the fine summit of Mount Massive right in front.

Soon we reached Healy Creek where it emerges from a narrow gorge, and crossed its double stream, the pedestrians having to clamber up behind the horsemen to make the passage dryshod. Leaving the broad, level valley of the Bow, and with it every trace of civilization for some days to come, we plunged into the ravine beside the swift, translucent river, until we mounted a very steep trail through thick forest and emerged high above the creek in a fine valley whence the retrospective views were very beautiful.

Our path led through a tract of burned and fallen timber to more open ground, trending steadily toward Simpson Pass, above which stood a gabled mountain, with a small glacier cradled on its bosom, against a gloomy, ominous background of dark and lurid clouds. The valley narrowed before us, well wooded near the torrent-bed. On one side rugged summits rose abruptly from the thickly timbered slopes; on the other, the more open alps, interspersed with belts and groves of trees, bare cliffs, and rocky terraces, merged into castellated peaks, the topmost crowned with snow.

As the evening shadows lengthened, before our camping ground was reached, strong gusts of wind came sweeping down the gorge, with driving rain beating pitilessly in our faces, but we pressed on until we found a pretty and fairly sheltered spot among the woods, where we pitched our tents.

A busy scene ensues. Peyto and Sinclair unload and attend to the horses; the guides are energetically employed cutting and collecting fuel; fire and water, the opening of boxes, and unpacking necessaries are my allotted share. In an incredibly short space of time the tents are up, the packs made snug, supper is ready, and we are all gathered round the blazing fire fully prepared to do ample justice to the bannocks and bacon and the huge saucepan full of steaming tea, under the black canopy of pines and almost darker sky.

Next morning we were off at half-past seven, in fair weather, though the trees and undergrowth were dripping.

We crossed the stream and, after twenty minutes' gradual ascent, diverged from the main trail to Simpson Pass and followed a steep pathway to the south through thick firs up a narrow rocky canyon till we arrived in a beautiful open park. The carpet of luxuriant grass and mossy turf was sprinkled gayly, although September was upon us, with a wealth of flowers; dark groups of trees bordered the rich expanse and crowned the knolls that broke its surface here and there; and, on either hand, the green slopes, broken by picturesque rock outcrops, culminated in a line of rugged pinnacles.

The timberline is passed soon after, and we mount steadily to a breezy, undulating alp, green and flower-strewn, skirting the continental watershed, and bearing frequent pretty lakelets in the sheltered hollows. Ever and anon a deep gorge dips sharply toward the east or west, giving a glimpse of larger, wooded valleys, where Healy Creek and Simpson River run to join the Bow and Kootenay, and finally sink to rest in the waters of the rival oceans.

This upland route was taken by Mr. Wilcox on his second journey to Mount Assiniboine, and it is undoubtedly the finest way as well as probably the easiest and quickest, in spite of a terrific fifteen hundred feet of descent to the source of the Simpson River.

About ten o'clock, from a lofty ridge some two thousand feet above our camp, we caught our first glimpse of our objective peak, bearing from this point a remarkable resemblance to the Swiss Dent Blanche as it loomed through the slight haze, fourteen or fifteen miles away, dwarfing all the other points and ranges. An hour later, from the highest point upon our highland trail, about seventy-seven hundred feet above the sea, we obtained a still better view of the noble pyramid, towering above a blue-black ridge hung with white glaciers, which lay between us and its base.

Crossing and recrossing the "backbone of the continent," we skirted the walls of an imposing natural fortification, fully two thousand feet in height, and, passing under its frowning ramparts close to the shores of two or three small lakes, halted for lunch near a round pond, from which some ducks flew off at our approach, and which from the numerous tracks leading into and out of it, we christened "the Bears' Bathtub."

All this time the going had been good, and Peyto made the most of it, leading at a tremendous rate, with Sinclair driving on the pack animals, we poor two-legged tramps having to do our utmost to keep pace with them.

After lunch a new experience began, where we in turn had a conspicuous advantage—a tremendous drop (fifteen hundred feet in fifty-five minutes, packhorse time) into an extraordinarily steep, weird valley, narrow and fire-swept, its serried ranks of bare and ghostly poles backed by slopes of scanty grass and a tumultuous expanse of rough gray rocks and tongues of scree. Toward the lower end an intricate maze of fallen logs was encountered, through which Peyto steered the horses with marvellous skill and rapidity, until we gained the valley of the chief source of the Simpson River, barren and boulder-strewn, divided into rugged sections by great ridges traversing it from side to side. Bare, burned trees reared their gaunt stems about us, or, fallen, littered the valley-bed, where strawberries and raspberries, gooseberries and blueberries, grew in wild profusion.

Crossing several of the strange barrier ridges, we soon arrived at the head of the valley, a cul-de-sac, with a grand amphitheatre of precipices and abrupt acclivities, three hundred feet or more in height, blocking our way and towering above the rich green flat, on which we halted for a brief well-earned rest beside a tree-girt lakelet, fed by a fine cascade that leaped from the rim of the great cirque above.

A zigzag track conducted us to the lowest point of this imposing barrier, and a scene of indescribable bleakness burst upon our gaze. The sun was hidden by the gathering clouds and the leaden sky formed a fit background for the rock-bound basin at our feet, hemmed in by gray, ruined towers, from which wide belts and tapering tongues of tumbled scree streamed down among the bare poles of the stricken pines, with a tiny tarn, sombre and forbidding, in its depths.

It was a fitting prelude to the long valley on which we now entered. Here was the acme of sheer desolation. Green-gray rocks and stones were strewn and piled in wild confusion amid sparse, stunted pines and firs; crumbling, drab-coloured sidehills were lost in jagged, broken ridges and shattered pinnacles that loomed in sullen dullness against the mournful sky, while a light drizzle bathed the scene in gloomy haze. Here and everywhere along the route the dreary silence and the strange scarcity of living things—a notable characteristic of the Canadian Cordilleras—were very striking. The whistle of the marmot, the rare whir of grouse, a hawk or eagle, and a little bird or two, with the occasional tracks of bear or deer, marten or mountain goat, alone betrayed that the region is not quite bereft of life.

Thus we swung on mile after mile, till the melancholy conditions began to change: Grass and light undergrowth appeared, the clouds broke, and, as we neared a rocky lake, Mount Assiniboine came into view once more, about five miles ahead, grander than ever, and, in spite of evening gloom, showing some detail of its horizontal belts of cliff and smooth, shining icy slopes.

Then came park country, rich green pasturage and dark forest belts, with a winding coal-black streambed meandering in the most abandoned manner through it all; and above, on either side, sharp, serrated ridges, severed by wide passes to the Spray and Cross Rivers, converged in the mass of Mount Assiniboine.

Still on we tramp, weary but buoyed up by the knowledge that the goal is near. Darkness falls apace and

> *Far along*
> *From peak to peak, the rattling crags among,*
> *Leaps the live thunder! Not from one lone cloud,*
> *But every mountain now hath found a tongue.*

A most impressive welcome from the still unconquered mountain, but more sinister than those whose hopes depended on fine weather quite appreciated.

At length, at 7:20, our chosen camping ground was reached, sheltered by a grove of trees, beside a trickling rivulet with the dark waters of Lake Assiniboine just visible beyond.

This lake, one of a dozen or more that nestle close under the precipices of the giant peak, is nearly two miles long, and, like many others in the neighbourhood, is without a visible outlet. The waters seem to drain away through the loose limestone strata, and in some valley far below suddenly burst forth from a mysterious subterranean cavern, a full-grown stream. This we were able to observe for ourselves at the source of the main Simpson River, at the head of the cul-de-sac, some miles from the nearest body of water at a higher altitude sufficient to produce so large a flow.

The night was none too promising—warm and cloudy, with light showers at intervals and distant muttering thunder; and, although later on the stars came out, ominous clouds still hung heavy round the horizon. The silence was broken again and again by the rumble and crash of falling ice and stones from the glacier a mile away, which aided the anxiety concerning weather prospects to drive the slumber from our wearied frames.

Nevertheless we were early astir. The moon was shining fitfully athwart the clouds and lighting up our noble peak with silvery brightness. As the sun rose, we had an opportunity of studying the mountain. Our camp, at an elevation of about seventy-two hundred feet, lay near the shore of the lake, a long mile from the cliff over which the northern glaciers of Mount Assiniboine descend abruptly; three thousand feet above the glacier rises the mighty monolith, a relic of the Carboniferous age. Two jagged ridges trend sharply upward from the outlying spurs, until they meet in a dark rocky apex just below the glistening, snowy summit; between them lies the formidable northern face, set at a fearsome angle and banded with almost horizontal strata, which form an impressive alternation of perpendicular cliff belts and glassy slopes of ice. The lowest band is specially remarkable—a spectacular, striated wall of brilliant red and yellow rock, running apparently entirely round the mountain, and particularly striking where the erosion and disintegration of the ridges leave a succession of coloured spires and pinnacles, radiant in the glowing sunshine.

By the advice of Peyto, the only member of the party who had ever been near the peak before, we determined to make our attempt from the southwestern side; but, instead of taking the horses by the long and arduous route adopted by Mr. Wilcox and Mr. Bryant on the occasion of their last attack, I conceived the plan of crossing the outlying spurs at a high altitude on foot from the usual base camp, believing that some way, for practiced mountaineers at least, could be discovered whereby the farther side might be reached and an open bivouac be made a starting point next morning, if it proved too long or difficult a task to gain the summit in a single day.

Being wholly unaware of the character of the mountain on the hidden side, and anticipating considerable difficulty in getting to the southwestern ridge, by which we hoped to reach the point where the last climbers were compelled to halt, we had little expectation of being successful on the first day, particularly as the nights were closing in at a comparatively early hour. So off we started at six o'clock—Peyto, Häsler, Bohren, and I—laden with two days' provisions, minor changes of raiment, blankets, and a light tent for the night, besides the usual camera and sundry other paraphernalia.

Twenty minutes' walk along the green flat brought us to the first snow, and a steep pull up hard snow slopes and a craggy wall of rock, followed by an awkward scramble over loose debris, landed us at half-past seven on the ice above. The glacier, covered with congealed snow and thin moraine, stretched away before us at an easy angle, with the great peak towering aloft upon our left. As we moved rapidly along I took the opportunity to scan with interest and curiosity the peculiar characteristics of that remarkable face, but the result of my observations was locked securely in my breast and not revealed until, on the following afternoon, we stood upon the crest above.

Forty minutes of quick walking took us to the summit of the sharp ridge which forms the skyline to the west and merges in the main northwestern arête. Two hundred feet below us lay another glacier, and away to our left a second pass, at the base of the great western ridge. Dropping down to the ice, we followed up the glacier, zigzagging to avoid the large crevasses, to the narrow little pass, which we reached at nine o'clock and found ourselves about ninety-six hundred feet above the sea and twenty-four hundred feet above the camp.

From this point the lower portion of the unknown side of our mountain lay in full view, and, to our joy, we saw that the anticipated difficulties were nonexistent. A comparatively easy traverse, along narrow but ample ledges covered with snow and debris, across the ribs and stony gullies which seamed the southwestern face, would bring us, with scarcely any loss of elevation, to the southwest ridge, whence the climb proper was expected to begin. Each of the gullies seemed to be a much-used channel for stones and ice and snow, and was of excessive steepness, so no inducement was offered to try an upward route nearer than the line that Mr. Wilcox took in his ascent from the valley. Below the horizontal ledge of the proposed traverse, the mountain shelved steeply down in long expanses of loose stones and snow, with not a little ice, into the depths of the contracted valley far beneath, containing the inevitable lakelet.

To counteract, however, this piece of unexpected good fortune, the light fleecy clouds, which had been hovering over the lower western peaks and growing larger and denser every hour, were blotting out the view and soon enveloped us in their chill embrace. With little hope of a successful ascent, we nevertheless made our way to the ridge, where we cached our blankets, tent, and the bulk of the provisions and, after a second breakfast, continued our upward progress at about half-past ten.

Our circle of vision dwindled from one hundred yards to fifty at the most; a steady drizzle, mingled with sleet, began to fall as we climbed cliff and ledge and gully, loose rocks and slopes of debris, as each appeared through the mists in front of us; and every few yards we built a little pile of stones to guide us in returning.

At length, at about 10,750 feet altitude, out of the gloom a mighty wall, seventy or eighty feet in height, loomed before us, its top lost in the clouds. The face seemed sheer, and actually overhung in places. None of us had ever seen this side of Mount Assiniboine, excepting Peyto, who had left us a short distance below to prospect for minerals, and we knew not where the summit lay. Of course we went first in the wrong direction. Imagining that this belt was as unbroken here as on the northern face, we sought a cleft up which to clamber and skirted the base to the right till we were brought up by a tremendous precipice some six thousand feet in depth. We had suddenly reached the edge of a gigantic buttress, where its converging sides met at an abrupt angle. Before us, and on either hand, was empty space, and at our feet a seemingly unbroken drop thousands of feet deep.

Behind rose the sharp edge of rock like polished masonry. Below the stony ledge by which we had approached, the mountainside shelved to the south in rugged steepness into far-distant gloom; and as we peered with caution round the angle, the farther side disclosed a most appalling face of black, forbidding precipice, one of the finest and most perpendicular it has been my lot to see.

Here for some moments I stood in solemn awe, perched like a statue in a lofty niche, cut in the topmost angle of a vast, titanic temple, with space in front, on either side, above, below, the yawning depths lost in the wreathing mists that wrapped the mountain's base.

Our progress in this direction barred, we now retraced our steps and spied a little rift by which, in spite of a fair overhang for the first twelve or fifteen feet, thanks to firm hand- and footholds, we were enabled to scramble to the summit of the cliff. Working to the left by a steep succession of ledges and clefts, we reached a narrow, broken ridge running upward from the west, with a sheer drop upon the farther side. We thought that we had struck the main western arête (for it is very difficult to locate one's self in a dense mist, especially upon an unknown mountain where we expected to find a regular three-sided cone) and followed its lead, till in ten minutes, to our great amazement, we found ourselves upon a peak! Narrow ridges descended to the east and west, the steep face of our ascent lay to the south, while upon the northern side a mighty precipice fell away virtually perpendicularly for thousands of feet, broken only by a short buttress, with equally sheer walls and edged with jagged pinnacles.

This "Lost Peak" was to us most mysterious. It seemed a genuine summit, narrow and pointed though it was, in altitude a trifle over eleven thousand feet. Yet where upon the mass of Mount Assiniboine was such a peak? We had imagined that the giant tooth rose more or less symmetrically on every side and judged the back ridge by the two that we had seen. Häsler at first insisted that we were on the veritable summit, but the elevation and configuration of our whole environment demolished such a theory. We strained our eyes; but, though the breeze kept the thick clouds in constant motion, we could not see more than about a hundred yards ahead. We shouted in this direction and in that; but our voices died away into space until at last held by some loftier mass, which echoed back an answer from the direction whence we had just come! Then we knew that we were standing upon the southeastern ridge, which must be longer and less steep, at any rate in its upper portion, than any of the others, and possess a distinct minor peak, separated from the main summit by a considerable break.

Such proved to be the case. After an hour spent in the cold and wet, striving to pierce the clouds, hoping some stronger current of wind might waft them off, and thus enable us to see the top and give us some idea of its character and how we might approach it, we built a "stone man" to commemorate our visit and, at half-past one, returned along the west arête until a chasm yawned beneath our feet—how deep we could not tell (it proved about two hundred feet)—and forced us to descend by our cliff route and down the crack to the base of the big wall. A few minutes going in the opposite direction brought us to a broad snow couloir, where the cliff receded and trended upward to the gap into which we had been gazing from above not long before, and away upon our left stretched the steep face of the great peak itself.

It was now too late to think of climbing farther, so we descended rapidly and rejoined Peyto near the cache. Here, during a meal, we held a council of war, and came to the unanimous determination to shoulder our packs and return to camp; feeling that, if the morrow were wet, we should be better off there, and if fine, it would take but little longer to come round in light marching order from the north than to make the ascent thus far with heavy packs from the tree line. In spite of a very speedy return, night fell upon us before we had quite descended the cliff wall below the northern glacier, and we stumbled into camp in black darkness about a quarter-past eight.

The clouds had begun to dissipate toward sunset; later on the moon rose in a clear, star-spangled sky; and the chill of frost augured favourably for our second campaign.

September 3rd, a notable date for us and Mount Assiniboine, dawned brilliantly. At ten minutes past six our little party of three set out from camp in the best of spirits, encouraged by the hearty good wishes of the packers, and made rapid progress by the route of the previous day. In two and a half hours we were on the second pass, enjoying this time a wide view to the south and the northwest of an expanse of indented mountain ranges and deep yawning valleys, with a little lake far below in every gorge. A brief halt here, and then on to the southwestern ridge, reaching the cache three and a quarter hours from the start. Upward, past the coloured belt, to our great cliff of yesterday. There, at half-past ten, we turned off to the left and crossed the couloir, full of deep snow upon an icy basis.

Beyond it lay the final thousand feet of the great mountain, its steep and rugged face a series of escarpments broken by tiny ledges and occasional sharp pinnacles, and rent at distant intervals by clefts and crevices nearly vertical. Slopes of solid ice or ice-hard snow, demanding arduous step-cutting, intervened below each wall and ledge and filled each cavity. The rocks were very brittle and extremely insecure, and to the ordinary difficulties there was added that abomination of the mountaineer, verglas, the thin coating of ice upon the rocks from the night's frost after the rain and sleet of yesterday.

The general line was diagonally across the face, but frequent minor consultations were required, the problems of immediate procedure being numerous.

Steadily onward the little party made its cautious way across these difficult approaches: ever on the alert, hand and foot alike pressed into service, each hold fully tested before the weight was trusted to it. A slippery ledge demanded an ignominious crawl; a series of gymnastic efforts were required to surmount some of the straight-up rocks and buttresses, where holds were few and far between. Detours were frequent to avoid impossible conditions; all sorts of cracks and crevices had to be utilized; and icy rifts were sometimes the only avenues of access to the tops of smooth, unbroken cliffs.

Thus step by step the advance continued, till, after a final scramble up a gully lined with solid ice and almost as steep and narrow as a chimney, we stood triumphantly upon the south arête, the summit in full view not more than three hundred feet above, reached by an easy ridge of snow, and Mount Assiniboine we knew was ours.

The strangest feature of the ascent lay in the fact that now for the first time we saw the actual summit, as the cliffs rose so steeply during our approach that we could never see more than a short distance beyond us.

White, vaporous clouds had been slowly drifting up for the last hour, and, fearing a repetition of the previous day's experience and the loss of the view, we hurried to the top, pausing only for a few moments to enjoy the panorama, to renew our acquaintance with our "Lost Peak," now five hundred feet below us, and to take a picture through the mist of the white summit, with its splendid eastern precipice.

A quarter of an hour sufficed to complete our victory, and at half-past twelve we stood as conquerors 11,860 feet above the sea (government survey altitude from distant bases), on the loftiest spot in Canada on which a human foot had then been planted.

The summit is a double one, crowned with ice and snow, the two points rising from the extremities of an almost level and very narrow ridge 150 feet in length, at the apex of the sharp arêtes from north and south. On the western side snow slopes tilted downward at a very acute angle, while on the east a stupendous precipice was overhung by a magnificent succession of enormous cornices from which a fringe of massive icicles depended.

One at a time—the other two securely anchored—we crawled with the utmost caution to the actual highest point and peeped over the edge of the huge, overhanging crest, down the sheer wall to a great, shining glacier six thousand feet or more below.

The view on all sides was remarkable, although the atmosphere was somewhat hazy and unsuitable for panoramic photography. Perched high upon our isolated pinnacle, fully fifteen hundred feet above the loftiest peak for many miles around, below us lay unfolded range after range of brown-gray mountains, patched with snow and sometimes glacier-hung, intersected by deep chasms or broader wooded valleys. A dozen lakes were counted, nestling between the outlying ridges of our peak, which proudly stands upon the backbone of the continent, and supplies the headwaters of three rivers—the Cross, the Simpson, and the Spray.

Far away to the northwest, beyond Mount Ball and the Vermilion Range, we could descry many an old friend among the mountains of the railway belt—Mount Goodsir and the Ottertails, Mount Stephen and Mount Temple, with the giants of the Divide, Mount Victoria, Lefroy, Hungabee, and a host of others, a noble group of striking points and glistening glaciers.

The main ridge northward, after a sharp descent of fifty feet, falls gently for a hundred yards or so, and then makes a wild pitch down to the glaciers at the mountain's base. When we arrived at this point (only through my most strenuous insistence, for the guides were anxious to return at once by the way we came), we looked down on the imposing face that is perhaps Assiniboine's most characteristic feature.

On the right the drop is perpendicular, a mighty wall with frequent overhanging strata and a pure snow curtain hanging vertically beneath the crowning cornice. But the north face, though not so sheer or awesome, is perhaps still more striking and unique. The shining steeps of purest ice, the encircling belts of time-eroded cliffs, sweep downward with tremendous majesty. Between the two a ragged ridge is formed, narrow and broken, like a series of roughly fractured wall ends.

As we gazed, the scheme that had been simmering in my brain since I looked upward to these heights the previous morning seemed more than ever practicable and at last found utterance: "Could we not manage to get down this way?" and the hope of crowning the triumph by a traverse of the mountain, conquering its reputed inaccessible ramparts (and that, too, in a descent), together with the prospect of an absolutely first-class climb, decided the reply in the affirmative. True, at least three great bands of rock lay there below us, any one of which might prove an insurmountable obstacle and necessitate a retracing of our footsteps, with the probable consequence of a night out, at a considerable altitude, among the icy fastnesses; but we had found some crack or cranny heretofore in their courses on the farther side, and—well, we would try to find an equally convenient right of way on this face, too.

So, after a halt of nearly two hours, at 1:40 we embarked upon our final essay.

Well roped and moving generally one at a time, we clambered downward foot by foot, now balancing upon the narrow ridge, five thousand feet of space at our right hand; then scrambling down a broken wall end, the rocks so friable that handhold after handhold had to be abandoned, and often half a dozen tested before a safe one could be found; now, when the ridge became too jagged or too sheer, making our cautious way along a tiny ledge or down the face itself, clinging to the cold buttresses, our fingers tightly clutching the scant projection of some icy knob, or digging into small interstices between the rocks; anon, an ice slope had to be negotiated with laborious cutting of steps in the hard wall-like surface; and again, cliff after cliff must be reconnoitred, its slippery upper rim traversed until a cleft was found and a gymnastic descent affected to the icebound declivity that fell away beneath its base.

For close upon two thousand feet the utmost skill and care were imperative at every step; for scarcely half a dozen could be taken in that distance where an unroped man who slipped would not inevitably have followed the rejected handholds and debris that hurtled down in leaps and bounds to crash in fragments on the rocks and boulders far below.

But with a rope a careful party of experienced mountaineers is absolutely free from danger; and, though it took our usually rapid trio three and a half hours to descend some eighteen hundred feet, our confidence was fully vindicated, for nothing insurmountable obstructed our advance, and, after a brief halt below the last cliff wall (where sundry relics of the Walling expedition were observed), a gay descent, on snow that needed no step-cutting, brought us soon after six o'clock to easier, continuous rocks, where we unroped.

A speedy spell swinging down rocks, with an occasional glissade, landed us on the glacier in forty minutes, and an hour later, in the gathering darkness, we approached the camp, after an absence of thirteen hours and a half, greeted by shouts of welcome and congratulation from Peyto and Sinclair (who had seen us on the summit) and strains of martial music from the latter's violin.

Before turning in, we took a last look at the splendid obelisk above us, radiant in the moonlight against the dark star-strewn canopy of heaven. A last look it proved; for next morning we awoke to a white world, with nothing visible of Mount Assiniboine but an occasional glimpse, through sweeping, leaden clouds, of its steep flanks deeply covered with the freshly fallen snow.

The return journey was begun at one o'clock that afternoon, and Desolation Valley was traversed in the snow and rain, our chill encampment being made in the flat pasture at the head of Simpson Valley.

Next day we made a most tremendous march in the teeth of a driving snowstorm. The valley, with its gaunt, spectral tree trunks, was drearier and more weird than ever; the blackened timber, outlined against the dazzling snow, showed in a mazy network; the bushes, with their load of fruit, peeped out forlornly amid their wintry environment, and every flower bore a tiny burden on its drooping head. The steep ascent of fifteen hundred feet was made in ever-deepening snow, and on the alp above we met the fierce blasts of the keen north wind, sweeping across the unprotected uplands. Wearied with our forced marches and two long days of arduous climbing, the tramping through soft, drifting snow, the steady upward trend of our advance, and the hard conflict with the driving storm, it was with deep relief that we crossed the final ridge and could descend to calmer regions through the dark, snow-laden pines. Still on we went, down Healy Creek to the Bow Valley, where the packers camped with their tired horses, and the guides and I tramped on two hours more to Banff, arriving there just five days and five hours from the time of our departure.

Our toils were over. In spite of adverse weather conditions, the expedition had been intensely interesting from start to finish, and more than a success from a climber's point of view; and the fact that the ascent was made upon the last possible day the weather would permit that season gave a dramatic touch that added an extra spice of satisfaction to the accomplishment of a mountaineering feat, perhaps the most sensational then achieved in North America.

THE BLACK CANYON WITH KOR (1976)

Pat Ament

Author's note: This piece was one of my first attempts at writing. I was a beginner, and I look through the article and can see hundreds of things I wish I had done differently. Yet my creative energies were primed and ready to do something "different." I had been reading Poe's long narrative about the adventures of Arthur Gordon Pym, and it occurred to me to style my language like Poe's, namely to overdramatize the wording. Maybe in Poe's day, that was not overdramatization. The exercise seemed to allow me to capture the madcap nature of my tall, invincible friend and also the pathetic partner, the "Pym," to whom he was roped. Almost everyone, to my surprise, loved this piece, and it would later prove a classic to be published in various anthologies—even a Czechoslovakian book, the author of whom said his readers felt it was the best piece in the book. At first, though, when this piece came out in Mountain magazine in England, one or two individuals thought I had committed some sacrilege upon the sacred image of their hero Kor. At the time, back in the 1960s, Layton himself was a bit sensitive and self-conscious and didn't much care for descriptions of himself with dirt in his teeth and hair pointed everywhere. I don't think he wanted to believe he had imposed his will a bit unfairly upon me. I think he now can laugh a little more and is able to realize what I wrote was an accurate portrait more than a caricature. Those were

The "Black"

days not to be forgotten, to be under the spell of such a powerfully upward-focused being, and I a mere immature tyro.

I . . . let myself down rapidly, striving by the vigor of my movements to banish the trepidation which I could overcome in no other manner . . . But presently I found my imagination growing terribly excited by thoughts of the vast depths yet to be descended. It was in vain I endeavored to banish these reflections and to keep my eyes steadily bent upon the flat surface of the cliff before me. The more earnestly I struggled not to think, the more intensely vivid became my conceptions, and the more horribly distinct. At length arrived that crisis of fancy, so fearful in all similar cases, the crisis in which we begin to anticipate the feelings with which we shall fall—to picture to ourselves the sickness, and dizziness, and the last struggle, and the half swoon, and the final bitterness of the rushing and headlong descent. And now I found these fancies creating their own realities, and all imagined horrors crowding upon me in fact. I felt my knees strike violently together, while my fingers were gradually but certainly relaxing their grasp. And now I was consumed with the irrepressible desire of looking below. I could not, I would not, confine my glances to the cliff; and, with a wild, indefinable emotion, half of horror, half of a relieved oppression, I threw my vision far down into the abyss. For one moment my fingers clutched convulsively upon their hold, while, with the movement, the faintest possible idea of ultimate escape wandered, like a shadow, through my mind—in the next my whole soul was pervaded with a longing to fall . . .

—EDGAR ALLAN POE

The passage of Poe's from his tale of Arthur Gordon Pym, brings to mind certain feelings which I had the misfortune—or fortune—to experience in the Black Canyon of the Gunnison at age seventeen under the unique guidance of Layton Kor, my climbing partner, who at that time was twenty-five. The adventure was a complete fiasco and has become somewhat of a legend amongst older climbers. The story has undoubtedly been exaggerated and capriciously altered over the years, but it nevertheless retains without error the underlying fact that an extraordinary, absurd, humorous, stupid, and altogether dangerous ordeal took place. It is with partial guilt, partial urging of conscience, and a desire to reveal one perspective of vintage Kor that I give this pseudo-Poe narrative of the unsuccessful trip to, and our preposterous flail upon, the walls of Colorado's Black Canyon.

Layton had recovered instantaneously from an unbelievable, backwards, head-over-heels leader fall off the Bastille Crack in Eldorado. My hands, however, were blistered nearly shut from the serious rope burns I had suffered catching him. I had been warned by a doctor to stay away from rock for at least a month, as the blisters were in danger of becoming infected, but Layton was impatient and wanted to depart immediately for the Black Canyon. He showed me a fuzzy snapshot of a two-thousand-foot vertical and overhanging wall called the Chasm View and reassured me that I was tough. I wanted to be with him, and Layton's wide eyes and warm laugh were very persuasive. Just the thought of such a first accent was enough to take my mind off the burns and diminish, in my idiocy and immaturity, all pain.

It was the middle of summer, and the three-hundred-or-so-mile drive from Boulder was hot. The old, blue Ford had four bald tires, and Kor gunned it up to eighty miles an hour most of the way. His eyes bulged and face contorted as he drove. His huge form leaned over the steering wheel, and he gazed nervously ahead. He held a peanut butter sandwich between his long legs and knobbly knees and shook to the tune of rock and roll which blasted out of the radio. I sat gripping the seat, making peanut butter sandwiches at Kor's command and, at one point, agreeing to take part in a handshake contest. There were two hundred pounds backing up his grip and about a hundred and thirty behind mine. My blisters burned at the thought, and I was squeezed out like a flame. A poor, hapless chipmunk was flattened while attempting to cross the highway.

The final part of the drive was a fifty-mile dirt road above cliffs and steep drops, which were the beginning of the Black Canyon. I was terrorized by this road, its unending, sharp curves, and the drag racer behind the wheel. I couldn't chew or swallow, and a lump of laughter and peanut butter stayed in my mouth for what seemed like an hour.

We arrived at the north rim of the canyon late in the day, parked, and, after a brief walk, were able to peer down our wall. The eerie, distant roar of the Gunnison River, which flowed far below, combined with the peculiar, lonely fragrance of sage, the desertlike silence, and hot wind, began to stir in me a fear of the remote area. My heart sank at the thought of having to catch another Kor fall or of encountering one of the huge, horribly rotten, sickly pink pegmatite bands which Layton had, during the drive, described with dread and superstition.

Layton snatched me up into his arms, pretending to have gone mad and to want to throw me over the edge. His fun was soon over, for I shot away from the exposed place like a rabbit, desperate to escape his mock chuckles. I endeavored to console myself, returned, and was from then on prepared to bear with personality and fortitude all further absurdity which was destined to occur.

After briefly exploring a steep, alien gully, which appeared superficially to be a feasible descent route into the canyon, we spent a bad night on the rim. It was anticipation of the climb that kept us awake, also hunger. We had practically depleted our supply of bivouac food—the peanut butter—and would have been foolish to break into the small ration of meat which Layton had brought in addition. Kor was immensely energetic and would not be discouraged by heat or hunger. Conspiring to stimulate me in the morning with a cup of boiling tea, he exploded his small stove and nearly burned down a picnic table. This put him in a bad humor, and he stared at me with a look as insidious as a sly sun which rose and began drawing the first beads of sweat from my forehead. We sorted pitons, slings, and carabiners, loaded bivouac gear into a large haul bag, filled a couple of water bottles, stuffed bolts and provisions into an old pack, and headed off to descend the steep gully.

He was obsessed. He wanted to get at it, to purge his soul on rock. He loved to go out on a limb, to be cleansed and dirtied by the deep shade and undiscerning power of his singular, high asylums. A sensation of emptiness, almost anger, flowed through me, as I questioned my role in the game. All doubt, all shadow, fell prey to fear—fear of Kor! He stared at me silently.

My thoughts were with facing the fear, with moving into Layton's world. I needed to discover life, to help find this route, and, if necessary, be led blindly by the master. The descent was hideous! The sultry gully into the canyon was filled with soil and sticker bushes. Small whimpers in a fretful, broken voice were my sound of protest. Proceeding down into the expanse of the gully, we found it to be suffocating. It was a treacherous sort of chute, eventually becoming slippery walls on all sides. Layton had loaded onto me what seemed an enormous amount of rope and hardware—plus the old pack. It was not easy to breathe with slings choking me and pack straps tearing at my shoulders. It felt unfair.

The heat was unbearable. An hour into the morning, I was ready to consume our entire two-day supply of water in a sitting. I was anxious, watching Kor climb without a belay. He moved smoothly down the precipitous, slabby walls of the gully. The weight upon my shoulders and around my neck made it impossible to follow without great strain. At one difficult section, a tiny slip would have meant a fall of about eight hundred feet. This took a lot out of me, and I worked up a horrible sweat. My burned hands stung as they scraped across crystals. I listened to the river crashing over boulders below, and the sound slashed at my thoughts. I groped at loose flakes, contemplating the anguish of one coming off in my hand. I wanted to do well, to win respect, to cling successfully to Kor's dream. My muscles quivered, and the moves were hazy before my eyes. Layton lowered himself down bulges, over ledges, and around bizarre heaps of gravel. He descended confidently, having no trouble with his load and ignoring my struggles. He was full of hope. I was a scorpion. Light gray rock, the blue flame of the sky, and a rainbow of images were the kaleidoscopic fluid of the search. The peculiar, personal release and lunacy of seeking out danger seemed a reward of disputable value.

Layton was for a moment outside his utopianism and thirsty but could not relax for thinking about getting to the base of the route. He carried the bottles of water in the haul bag, and I prayed that he would save a sip. I licked the parched lining of my mouth. Who was this maniac? Why was I permitting myself to go along with him?

At last, we were at the base of the route, dripping with sweat and trying to solve the puzzle of rope and snarl of slings which bound me like a fairy-tale squid. My hands were soft and white, oozing with puss which drained from a couple of broken blisters. Kor allowed me a swallow or two of water, which only antagonized my thirst, then tied in and led upward. A towering illusion, tall as a man, with white T-shirt and pants, long socks, and *kletterschuhe*, hung on an overhang above my head. The jeweled light of the sun scorched my thoughts. I had, above me, a kind of surrealism—a creature whose ability on rock matched my vision—Layton Kor, spread-eagled and silhouetted, his senses suspended momentarily but bodily powers frenzied. I squeezed the rope, then fed it out as he led swiftly up a difficult crack. The man was driven, afraid to fall, afraid to fail, tormented, all-powerful in a search for rich experience. He ascended with imagination, inclined to go the hard way when a choice existed, tense, uneasy, jumpy, jittery, critical, happy. He was awesome—more so than the wall—and disappeared up into the lair of an overhang. I sat like a piece of cactus, sweltering, stifled in a furnace of talus, awaiting the restless cry, "Come on up!" The river was 150 yards below and glistened even in the shadows. Scrambling down to it for a cold drink was an idea dismissed in view of the uphill hike back.

He was too big for belay ledges and looked uncomfortable hooked into one. As I followed the pitch, attacking strenuous pulls and long reaches, I discovered that my worst opponent was the old pack. While thinking I was in perfect balance, I would start to fall backwards and would expend precious energy recovering. My hands were a mess, and it was difficult even to hold a piton hammer—much less pound out pins. I was unable to retrieve the first piton, although I worked at it to the point of exhaustion. I was convinced that Layton had overdriven the thing and so left it. I began to feel extremely insecure and yelled for tension. I received slack. The lack of communication was frustrating, and my yells were overruled by the superior authority of the river. When I reached Layton, he asked, "You get that pin out?" I trembled and replied, "I have it here somewhere." He complained of aching feet and insisted on doing the next lead. I was too busy contemplating my lie to argue, so belayed. He stemmed over an impressive overhang and vanished into the heights. The route seemed to have been built for Kor, because I found the holds always out of reach. Layton suggested I take the third lead. It was an incentive to forget for a while the sorry state of my palms. The hammer was too painful to hold, but the rock relented momentarily, so I was able to climb unprotected to a stance about one hundred feet straight up. Kor was impressed with this but irritated when I could not haul the bag. My hands simply couldn't take it. He hurried up the pitch, and we tugged at the clumsy duffel bag together. That was the end of my leading, I was informed.

It was at this point that war began. Suddenly and quite unexpectedly, Kor yelled, "Where's your hard hat?!" I answered, "My what?" He thrust a handful of rope against the wall with such force that I thought we would both fall off. He kicked the wall and, looking as if he was going to strangle me, shouted, "No one climbs in the Black Canyon without a hard hat!" I was so intimidated by this outburst that I failed to notice he was not wearing one either. I indiscreetly let pass, at this moment, a bit of silent although untimely flatus of so foul and putrid an odor that all oxygen was removed from the vicinity of our perch. It took but an instant (which seemed an eternity) for the very bad message to reach Kor's nose. Now, I almost unroped with the intention of jumping rather than face the frightful demon who stood gagging so near at hand. He hovered over me, his face puffing with rage. He let out a chilling scream and raced up the wall, not bothering to place pitons where he knew I would need them. I nearly vomited when he thrust himself into a ferocious, dizzy, overhanging crack and forced his way up it with rope and haul line dangling down to me like cobras.

All flexibility had gone out of my fingers. I removed the pack and set it atop the haul bag, which sat comfortably on the stance without an anchor. It was surely one hundred degrees F, and my thirst was intolerable. I forced a hand and arm into the bag and pulled out a bottle. While belaying with one hand, I twisted the top off with my teeth and began to guzzle. The tone of the climb had changed so radically that I felt faint. A muted "off belay" from above told me that I had best get the bottle back into the bag fast. Stealing water might be punishable by more unprotected leading. As I fumbled with the bottle and bag, the haul line grew tight, and, just as the bottle disappeared into the opening, up went the big bag with my pack teetering, to my horror and dismay, on top where I had set it. The heavy bundle remained intact and was dragged over a bulge and up into a place hidden from my view where, by all indications, Kor was losing his mind with anger. "Oh my God, my arms are numb," he raved.

I had to keep my wits about me. A display of skill, I thought, might save me from the wrath of the fiend above. But it was all I could do to gain an inch on the pitch without tension. I very skillfully wore my voice out bellowing for the tight line. My hands were two blobs of dirt, puss, and shredded skin. "Heel and toe," Kor shrieked. I was encouraged, but slipped several feet down, trying to figure out what he meant.

At the belay, he had regained his composure but did not speak to me. We hung from slings attached to two feebly placed knifeblade pitons which Layton was eager to get away from. A severe chimney became the object of his study. He would climb it conscientiously, I reasoned, for there was no desire to die here, was there? I was delirious and needed water. Adrenaline flowed and, as I found myself somehow following the obstacle—the 5.10 crack-chimney affair—I was bewildered and inspired by techniques which I had applied but did not understand. There were expressions of struggle so deeply found that they would not transpire again. I became confused, drew upon untapped resources, and stretched my limbs through a hundred variations of divine bumbling. One thing was for sure: The pack and I would not both fit into the slot at once. Kor advised me to try the "Yosemite haul." I was to hook the pack to a long sling, then the sling to my waist loop, and drag the pack as it hung well below. I regretted tackling such a scheme, for it was 5.11 just getting the beast off my back. Then the buckles of the straps caught on every conceivable projection until I was certain that the tension from above and immovable weight below would tear me in half.

I somehow achieved Kor's position, after pulling and being hauled on the rope. Kor did not delay in leading up one more unbelievable, overhanging, obscure pitch. His tremendous skill was absolutely evident. It was easy to know why he was one of the great climbers of the world.

The pitch was all direct aid, and, Jumars (prusik handles) having not yet been invented, I thought I would die trying to reach from one carabiner to the next. As usual, Layton could not see me and was unable to determine whether my winded gripes were from falling, trying to get tension, or just pain. I would give each piton a halfhearted tap and grimace, before deciding that it was overdriven and a permanent fixture. I had no hands left, no voice, no spirit, only hope that we could bivouac, drink the water, and somehow rejuvenate. All the pitons stayed in, and I was ashamed but kept fighting.

As I drained the last of my will trying to surmount the belay ledge, I caught sight of my companion. Kor's hair pointed in every direction. His mouth and eyes were full of dirt. Sweat rolled down his cheeks. His famous buck teeth were the focus of an inimitable grin. He was a rebel with a bit of a temper, supremely talented, fueled by sheer force, set off from other climbers by a light—an illumination or charisma—and profound competence. He asked, "Did you get all the pins?" I had none with me but seemed to feel that the summit was near and that a few of the little iron strips would not be missed. I was unable to speak but simply nodded my head in the affirmative while reclining and gasping for air. We were seven hundred or more feet above the gully, a little less than halfway to the rim. Kor gave me a worried glance and observed, "You look bad, Ament. You're pale." He then ventured up onto the next formidable pitch, examining it for its artistic qualities.

What was I to do or say? I regarded life at that instant as an illness for which help was not available. I dreaded the thought of continuing but also feared retreat. Going down would mean Kor finding the pitons still in place. It would mean having to thrash our way back up the horrible gully. To my amazement, Kor returned and, with no explanation whatsoever, made preparations for rappelling. This abrupt decision on his part filled me with disconcerting questions. It was only later that I would know it had been Kor's genuine concern for my condition which turned him back. He placed a bolt, and I watched the small thing bend in its hole as he applied his weight to the rope. I listened to the tinging of metal against metal as he discovered and removed the pitons while on rappel. Small, indistinct curses drifted up to me and, finally, "Off rappel." I was sure that I would not be able to hold onto the rope—even with a brake bar—but resigned myself to trying. Layton kept guard over the rope ends, in case I decided to pick up speed. In the course of the rappel, my blisters became mangled cuts while sharp throbs pierced my cramped fingers.

Kor detested my lack of candor about the pitons, and so did I. That was half the hurt. His smiles gnawed at me with excruciating clarity. For an instant, he was understanding, and I remembered the other sides of him which existed—patient, insightful sides. My wretchedness and misery permeated the desolation of his stare, and my dejected state brought upon Kor an eagerness to escape the Black Canyon of the Gunnison and all of southwestern Colorado.

A quick, violent rainstorm gave us relief but was accompanied by several disturbing bolts of lightning and thunder crashes. After several agonizing rappels, we stood at the bottom in darkness. The ominous, forbidding, evil gully rose endlessly above. Melancholy of night and uncertainty filled the gully. Climbing insufficiently expressed, a poignant denouement and dismal disappointment, blameless loss with cruel psychic and emotional meaning, overcame me like the heat. I was unable to see the glorious images and romantic insights which, sometimes, rescue crucified minds from such drudgery and despair.

Kor withdrew upward into the night, leaving me to the demons of unbearable and unpredictable allusion, as well as with a rack of hardware and heavy, rain-drenched rope which I could barely lift. I had let my heart be molded by him and, strangely, knew that I would probably do so again. I loved Kor and hated him and in no way could deny either. The gully was a horrid task, and I was alone in it. Kor was somewhere far ahead, maybe almost up to the rim, possibly in pieces below. It was a vexed question, for it was I who had a "longing to fall."

I persevered toward a glimmer of sky, up steep slabs, through mud and stickers, over loose boulders, as if steering my bones through the grave, and clawing in the direction of a dim glow—the headlights of the Ford. My exertions became greater, I stumbled through sage, got into the car, shut the door, and fell asleep. Layton was determined to grind out the drive back to Boulder that night.

My eyes opened in the town of Gunnison. It was past midnight, we had stopped, and Kor stood outside rapping on the door of an A & W Rootbeer stand, which was closed. He looked like death and for all practical purposes frightened the janitor into letting him in. The fellow was obliged to fix the apparition a float! I went back to sleep. Was it really happening?

About an hour later, Layton pulled off onto what appeared to be a turnout, stopped, got out of the car, and threw his sleeping bag, me, and my sleeping bag into the dirt. There we slept for the rest of the night. At the crack of dawn, we made a quick dash to the Ford, delivering ourselves from a rancher's perverse sense of humor and two thousand hooves of five hundred cows being herded toward us.

Kor said nothing to me all the way home but, upon arriving in Boulder, reported voluntarily to a number of other climbers. His account of the ordeal was marked by a lack of particulars and was, simply, "Ament left all the pins in, so we had to come back." I recalled saving his life on the Bastille Crack in Eldorado and felt that he was being ungrateful. I began to realize how hard I had actually pushed on the wall of the Chasm View and in the exposed gully. Through young eyes and foolish insecurity, I saw Layton as the dishonest one . . . but, with a bit of reflection, returned to my senses. He had told the truth, really. I understood and forgave him for his madness. He had shown me the Black Canyon, perplexed me, and tortured my will and ego; but, following our adventure, he made plans to climb with me again in Eldorado, forgot for a while about the Chasm View, laughed, and, after all, was my friend.

OUT WITH THE BOYS AGAIN (1976)

Mike Thompson

Our leader had decreed that, in order not to place an intolerable burden upon the Nepalese countryside, we should
walk to base camp in two parties, one travelling a day behind
the other. Perhaps unwisely, he labeled these the "A team"
and the "B team," and immediately there was much specula-
tion as to the underlying basis for his selection. At first there
were fears among the B team that the choice of summiters
had already taken place and that they were travelling with
the leader in order that they could plot the fine details of
the assault in secrecy. But even the most paranoid could not
sustain this belief for long, and a more popular theory was
that the "chaps" were in the A team and the "lads" in the
B team. This perhaps was nearer the truth, since what had
happened was that Chris had, quite understandably, taken
with him all the executives: Sirdar Pertemba, base camp
manager Mike Cheney, equipment officer Dave Clarke,
senior doctor Charles Clarke, and of course the media in the
shape of the *Sunday Times* reporter and the television team.
These middle managers were, during their fortnight's walk,
to have the interesting experience of, in the words of Our
Leader, "being let in on his thinking." The B team, gloriously
free of logistics, planning, scenarios, computer printouts,

The Himalayas with Makalu on the right

communication setups, and the like, immediately sank into that form of communal warmth generated by squaddies in a barrack room, that impenetrable bloody-mindedness born of the I-only-work-here mentality of the shop floor. A series of perfectly sensible decisions led to the emphasis of a division that is always incipiently present in any large expedition. The A team represented the Overground Leadership, the B team the Underground Leadership.

In theory, we, the B team members, were in the tender care of the Deputy Dawg, Hamish MacInnes, but Hamish is never one to assert his authority unduly, and even if he had tried to he would have had to cope with that powerfully built and passionate anarchist, Doug Scott. One of the disadvantages of anarchy concerns decision making. For myself, I always feel that too much fuss is made about decisions on expeditions. There seems to me to be only one real decision, which is when that letter in unmistakeable scrawl arrives, saying: "How about coming on the coldest holiday of your life. PS: Will you do the food?" and like a fool you write back and say "Yes." But on the day the A team left Kathmandu, Deputy Dawg fell ill. Should we set off the next day as planned, leaving Hamish behind, or should we wait a few days to see if he recovered—a course of action (or, rather, inaction) that might also allow Martin Boysen, who had got his leg stuck in the Trango Tower, to catch up with us? Of course, Hamish himself should have taken the decision, but he, though unable to walk, refused to admit that he was ill. His Scottish stubborness is so highly developed that even if he had a leg amputated he would insist that it was just a slight limp. Not one of us was prepared to take that enormous step from private soldier to lance corporal, and make a decision, so several delightful days were passed in the fleshpots of Kathmandu until very early one morning some Land Rovers arrived at the hotel. They seemed to be for us, so we set off.

I suppose that during the approach we should have been organized by the second Sirdar, Ang Phu, but he had been having severe marital problems and was hitting the *chang* pretty hard, so we just wandered along, stopping where the Sherpas usually stopped, eating what *kancha* the cook gave us to eat, and generally building up a casual yet strong rapport with the Sherpas, by approving of their choice of campsites and menus, and by luring one another into wayside *chang* houses.

The members of the A team had adopted the puritanical regime of getting up in the morning, eating breakfast, and then walking until they got to the next campsite in the afternoon. We followed the more traditional pattern of just tea and biscuits in bed, followed by two or three hours' walk during the cool of early morning, until, rounding a corner, one came across the kitchen with its alfresco breakfast of pancakes, eggs, chips, cheese, tuna fish, tea, and chocolate biscuits, almost ready to serve. After this a little sleep and a gentle run-in through a few *chang* houses would bring us to the next campsite in the early afternoon. Of course there were occasional interruptions to the idyllic progress of this mobile, intensive-care geriatric unit, such as when Doug Scott was waylaid at a *chang* house by Ang Phu before the sun had even risen and never even reached the breakfast place, or when I foolishly followed Ned Kelly (who had been there before) and ended up in a trackless jungle and on the wrong side of a monsoon-swollen torrent.

The level of conversation was exceptionally high, by which I mean that we gave full rein to a very childish brand of humour, often in questionable taste. The greatest favourites were Whillans jokes. One could always tell when one of these was coming, as the teller would suddenly screw up his face, narrow his eyes to slits, and begin to emit a high-pitched whine. Useful on many occasions, to justify the imbalance between a porter carrying about seventy pounds and a sahib carrying his Olympus OM1 was: "No! No! These fellows are used to it—they've done it all their lives." Happy hours were passed recounting those epics in which Whillans would gradually unfold an account of his rectitude and forbearance in the face of seemingly intolerable chicanery and provocation. Like some Greek tragedy the sequence of events would move inexorably to the inevitable, fateful conclusion. All such tales led to the same final and literal punch line: "So I 'it 'im."

Hamish MacInnes recounted how, during Dr. Herrligkoffer's European expedition to the Southwest Face of Everest, Don, apart from nicknaming his leader "Sterlingscoffer," did in fact behave with astonishing forbearance in the face of almost unendurable provocation and never once stepped out of line—until the expedition was over.

Apparently, during the earliest stages of the expedition, when the members were just getting to know one another, they heard on the base camp radio that Germany had just beaten England in the World Cup. "Aha!" cried the dour Felix Kuen (the climbing leader) to Don. "We have beaten you at your national game!" Don paused, looked around, narrowed his eyes to the merest slits, leant forward, paused again, and said in a harsh whisper: "Aye, but we've beaten you at your national game twice now." No wonder the individualistic, subversive Whillans became the cult hero of the B team. Never was anyone more present by his absence.

The other great approach-march sport, I'm ashamed to say, was "Boardman-baiting." Poor Peter had recently been appointed to the post of Permanent Under-Secretary to the President of the National Amalgamated Union of Mountaineers of Great Britain and Bradford. What is more, he alone amongst us was being paid while on the expedition: somewhere, we believed, in the region of £30,000 per year of our, the taxpayers', money. The reality was barely less infuriating: He was the National Officer of the British Mountaineering Council (the BMC), which as you will all know is run by Dennis Gray, who, on several occasions (on the basis of his experience on some very large expeditions to quite small mountains), has attacked modest expeditions (including ours) to very large mountains as being counter to the proletarian ideology of the true heartland and fountainhead of British mountaineering—Yorkshire.

But perhaps, while on the subject of Yorkshire, I can digress for a moment, for we did have with us one Yorkshireman, Mike Rhodes (from Bradford, to boot). Mike had not, until Everest came along, travelled outside Yorkshire. After all, what is there outside Yorkshire worth travelling for? Whenever anything un-Yorkshire-like happened to him, such as being bitten by a leech, being offered curry and rice, spaghetti and Parmesan cheese or *chang*, or falling through a crevasse in the icefall, he would remark in a surprised and slightly pained voice: "Nothing like this in Bradford" (pronounced "Bratfud"). As Martin Boysen remarked, when he finally caught us up: "People are always going on about the dangers of professional mountaineers, but what about professional Yorkshiremen?"

But to return to Boardman-baiting: This would usually be initiated by some seemingly innocent enquiry such as, "What do you do all day in your office on the fiftieth floor of Dennis Gray Tower?" And then we would hear about all sorts of official bodies, such as the UIAA and the MLC board, about negotiations for access, about grant supports for students writing PhDs on climbing harnesses or crash-hats, and reading papers on specialized aspects of their research at international seminars in the Caucasus. All this was a revelation to me: I had been climbing all these years unaware of the existence of this bureaucracy, and it was all I could do to keep up with the initials and the jargon. Crags, I discovered, were "recreational facilities" and the BMC was empowered, if need be, to acquire these recreational facilities by compulsory purchase (CPO, you know). And all this time I'd thought they were crags!

> *Recreational Facility of Ages cleft for me*
> *Let me hide myself in Thee.*

Usually, by this time, Tut would be writhing on the ground in paroxysms of laughter, gasping: "PhDs on harness, BSI kite-marked nuts"; and Doug, fists clenched and beads of sweat standing out on his furrowed brow, would be dreaming of the not-too-far-off day when he would lead his first guerilla raid to blow up a National Park Information Centre; or the glorious morning when the newspaper headlines would shriek: "Stanage Warden Murdered By Inadequately Clad Climber."

If the baiting was taking place in a *chang* house, the chances were that it would really take off at this point, the British Mountaineering Council becoming one with the British Motor Corporation and Dennis Gray merging with Lord Stokes and being blamed for the state of the economy and for minivans breaking down on the M1. And then, in a desperate conciliatory gesture Peter would deliver the final stunning blow: "But we're doing all this on your behalf."

At Kunde, we momentarily met up with the A team. Though we were forced to attend an expedition meeting ("Welcome aboard" said Our Leader, adopting the terminology of the only one of the armed services of which he has not been a member) and to perform the more menial tasks of equipment issue and crampon adjustment, we did have the rare pleasure of watching Dave Clarke as he presided over the most depressing thing that can happen to any shopkeeper—the distribution of his entire stock without receiving a penny in exchange. There was a brief respite when we split again into A and B teams for the walk to base camp, but once there the Underground Leadership was totally submerged as the Logistic Machine swung into action—and very impressive action it was too! We got our kicks in the icefall—up at two in the morning and glissade down in time for breakfast—and did penance trying to break down the MacInnes boxes into thirty-pound loads: All the sections of the incredibly compli-cated aluminium frames were threaded together with elastic string, and, just as one coaxed the last bit into a large card-board box, another bit would escape and the whole frame would re-erect itself like a monstrous Jack-in-the-box. It was more than even Boysen's legendary patience could stand, and the Old Fox of Glencoe's ears must have been burning as, far above us in the Western Cwm, he indulged himself con-structing the highest truss-girder bridge in the world.

The Sherpas built a shrine to placate whatever it was that lived in the icefall and consecrated it with McVitie's choco-late wholemeal biscuits and John Haig whisky; and Mr. and Mrs. Boardman (Dim Juff, the Duff Doctor) excavated out-side their tent a patio-cum-sun-terrace, which, with its gen-teel folding chairs and sun-shaded table, might have passed unremarked on the Algarve but had a certain incongruity at eighteen and a half thousand feet on the Khumbu Glacier.

At this early stage of the climb there were far too many Chiefs and far too many Indians, and this, coupled with the fact that there was only one camp and that all the action took place within full view of it, meant that the traditional avenues whereby the Underground Leadership could assert its devious influence were firmly closed. Usually on such expeditions, the Overground Leadership can be contained by witchcraft accusations, of which the most feared (and therefore most effective) are "secret-eating" and "equipment-hoarding." "Unnatural sexual practices" is, by comparison, surprisingly ineffective. On the positive side, the Underground can, once the expedition is strung out over a number of camps and communications are strained, influence the course of events by withholding information. In this way the Overground still makes all the decisions, but on the basis of grossly inadequate information, and this means that, skillfully handled, the Overground without realizing it simply okays the wishes of the Underground. When communications are really stretched it may be possible to ignore the Overground completely and present them with, in Mick Burke's phrase, "a fait accompli, as they say in Spain." For this kind of action to be constructive in the long run, one needs a leader who changes his mind a lot and has difficulty in remembering from one day to the next what he has decided. We were fortunate in having such a leader.

Once on the face itself, the situation suddenly changed. It was like Annapurna again. All at once the expedition was quite small; there weren't enough people to do everything that had to be done, and one's own contributions and omissions were immediately evident to one's fellows. At last, this was what we had come for!

The fulfillment of long-cherished desires can take some curious forms at high altitude. As a "support climber," I was aware that I was fortunate to have got as far as becoming the Camp 4 Commandant, responsible, in theory, for five face boxes, an equipment dump, nine Sherpas, and a variable number of "lead climbers" in transit. I became obsessed with actually becoming a Sherpa, and increasingly I resented the lead climbers who passed through on oxygen carrying just their personal equipment. I was quite ridiculously touched when, having managed to drag myself and my load up to Camp 5 without oxygen, Pertemba said, with what I now suspect was heavy sarcasm: "You are a real Sherpa now."

Camp 5, perched in its little notch, was filled with slightly unbalanced euphoria. Our leader, doing his usual thing of shooting up to the front (and rightly so), had now entered his Mad Madhi phase, running out drums of fixed rope in the wrong direction, ranting on at Ang Phurpa about "really good Sherpa food," working out logistics on his porridge-encrusted electronic calculator, and communicating his befuddled instructions to the outside world on a broken walkie-talkie that had been persuaded to work again by jamming a ballpoint pen into its circuitry.

A few days later I, too, became a transit passenger and moved up to Camp 5 along with Dougal Haston, who was being whisked on oxygen from Camp 2 to Camp 5, like Lenin in his sealed train, to join Doug (who was resting on oxygen) for the first summit attempt. Still playing the Sherpa, I stopped off at the old Camp 4 site and spent a happy couple of hours excavating the Japanese peg-store (we had in fact run out of rock pitons). As I clanked into Camp 5, the triumphant Rock-Banders, Nick and Tut, came leaping down the fixed ropes (cries of "aye, aye, aye . . ." etc.) and there was Doug, the angst-ridden giant, happily sorting out the food and equipment for the summit bid. A changed man, he explained to me that, at the very moment when success was within our grasp, the impossible had happened: The Underground and the Overground had merged into a single upward-thrusting force. Miraculously free, for the moment, of Sandhurst-trained leaders and trades-unionized bureaucrats, at peace with the world, he could direct his all toward what Whillans would call: "T' job we've come 'ere for." He was his own man at last.

And he was right about the Leadership: Bonington and his image were now clearly separate, and all the logistics of climbing Everest were condensed into just six heavy loads which just six of us would have to carry through the Rock Band the next day to establish Camp 6. In the jargon of the sociologist, success on Everest requires massive redundancy, duplication, and overlap, but this was just what we didn't have. If just one of us didn't make it up the fixed ropes, then the summit bid would be off. What was more, the route through the Rock Band was not complete nor had a site for Camp 6 been found. Doug and Dougal would have to set off before us, complete the route, fix three hundred feet of rope, and find and excavate the site for their Summit Box. In consequence, it was a happy little nonredundant, unduplicated, nonoverlapping group that sat enjoying the view and the sunshine that afternoon in the little crow's nest that was Camp 6.

As is the way on such momentous occasions, the conversation was quite spectacularly inane: me getting at the technologically illiterate Dougal, who the evening before had omitted to turn on the oxygen bottle, with the result that we spent the whole night sucking the thin outside air through saliva-filled masks; Mick Burke remarking, "What a lovely spot for a bungalow"; and then Chris, after much deliberation, announcing, "You know, we must be the highest people on Earth." Since the Americans had just failed on K2, since there was no one on Kanchenjunga, and since we could see that there was no one on Lhotse, I suppose he was right and we were the highest people on Earth—but not for long! For, as we wished Dougal and Doug good luck and set off down the fixed ropes in the evening sunlight, I knew that for me Everest was over. Still, I consoled myself with the words of the great Maurice Herzog: "There are other recreational facilities in the lives of men."* (*I quote, of course, from the official translation of *Annapurna*, by P. Boardman, published by The Closed Shop Press, Bradford.)

GLOSSARY

abseiling: descending by sliding down a rope; see also rappelling.

aid: using means other than the actions of hands, feet, and body English to get up a climb.

aiguille: a sharp-pointed pinnacle of rock.

alcove: a belay ledge surrounded by vertical rock on all sides.

anchor: a means by which climbers are secured to a cliff; the point where the rope is fixed to the rock.

arête: a narrow ridge or an outside edge or corner of rock.

belay: procedure of securing a climber by the use of a rope.

belayer: the person at the belay station securing the climber.

bergschrund: the uppermost crevasse in a glacier.

beta: prior information about a climb, including sequence, rests, gear, clips, etc.

big wall: a long climb traditionally done over multiple days, but may take less time for ace climbers.

biner: see carabiner.

bivy: see bivouac.

bivouac: an uncomfortable sleeping place in the middle of a route; also called bivi.

bolt: an artificial anchor placed in a hole drilled for that purpose.

bomber: absolutely fail-safe (as in a very solid anchor or big, big handhold); sometimes called bombproof.

bombproof: see bomber.

bouldering: climbs at the base of a cliff or on small boulders to practice climbing skills performed without a belay rope, having just a mat to fall onto. Climbers do "boulder problems," where the solution is a series of moves that are repeated until the problem is accomplished.

bridging: see stemming.

buttress: an outside edge of rock that's much broader than an arête.

cagoule: a lightweight, weatherproof raincoat with a hood.

cam: to lodge in a crack by counterpressure; that which lodges.

carabiner: aluminum alloy rings equipped with a spring-loaded snap gate; sometimes called biners.

chalk: a compound, usually magnesium carbonate, used to improve grip on holds by absorbing sweat.

chimney: a crack of sufficient size to accept a climber's entire body.

chock: see nut.

chockstone: a rock lodged in a crack.

cirque: a deep, steep-walled basin on a mountain.

clean: routes that are variously free of vegetation or loose rock, or where you don't need to place pitons; the act of removing chocks and other gear from a pitch.

couloir: a steep mountainside gorge.

crimp: a grip where the first knuckle is extended, allowing the fingertips to rest on a small ledge while the second knuckle is flexed.

crimper: a small but positive edge.

crux: the most difficult move or sequence of moves on a climb, typically marked on topos with the difficulty rating.

deadpoint: the high position of a dynamic move where all motion stops for a moment.

dihedral: an inside corner of the climbing surface, formed by two planes of rock, like the oblique angle formed by the pages in an open book.

flash: free climbing a route from bottom to top on your first try, but with the aid of beta.

free climb: the upward progress gained by a climber's own efforts, using hands and feet on available features, unaided or free of attending ropes and gear. Rope is only used to safeguard against injury, not for upward progress or resting.

glissade: to slide down a steep slope of snow on one's rump or feet.

grade: a rating that tells how much time an experienced climber will take on a given climb; the "overall seriousness" grade (referring to the level of commitment, overall technical difficulty, ease of escape, and length of route), denoted by Roman numerals.

haul bag: a large and often unwieldy bag into which supplies and climbing equipment may be thrown.

heel hooking: the attempt to use the foot as a hand, usually on a vertical climb, where the heel is kicked over the head and hooked over a large hold.

hex: see hexentric.

hexentric: six-sided or barrel-shaped anchor that can be wedged into wide cracks and bottlenecks; sometimes called a hex.

jam: wedging feet, hands, fingers, or other body parts to gain purchase in a crack.

jug: a handhold that looks like a jug handle.

Jumar: a type of mechanical ascender; to ascend a rope using a mechanical ascender.

layback, laybacking: climbing maneuver that entails pulling with the hands while pushing with the feet; also called lieback.

lead: to be the first on a climb, belayed from below, and placing protection to safeguard a fall.

lieback, liebacking: climbing maneuver that entails pulling with the hands while pushing with the feet; also called layback.

lock-off: a single handhold with enough strength to allow the other hand to shift to a new handhold.

move: one of a series of motions necessary to gain climbing distance.

mountaineering: reaching mountaintops using a combination of skills (such as rock climbing and ice climbing).

multi-pitch: a climb that takes more than one rope-length.

nut: a wedge or mechanical device that provides secure anchor to the rock; sometimes called a chock.

off-width: a crack that is too wide to use as a finger, hand, or fist jam but too narrow to get right inside and climb as a chimney.

on-sight: to successfully climb a route without prior knowledge or experience of the moves.

peg: see piton.

perlon: a material used in accessory cord.

pitch: the section of rope between belays.

pin: see piton.

piton: metal spikes of various shapes that are hammered into the rock to provide anchors in cracks; sometimes called pins or pegs. These types of anchors were common in the 1970s but are not used today.

placement: the position of a nut or anchor.

pocket: a hole or cavity in the climbing surface used as a hold.

portaledge: a deployable hanging tent system designed for rock climbers who spend multiple days and nights on a big wall climb.

protection: the anchors used to safeguard the leader; sometimes called pro. Until the 1970s, protection devices were almost exclusively pitons—steel spikes that were hammered into cracks in the rock. Since then, various alloy wedges and intricate camming devices have virtually replaced pitons as generic protection devices. These wedges and cams are fitted into hollows and constrictions in cracks, and when fallen upon actually wedge farther into the rock. In the absence of cracks, permanent bolt anchors are drilled and fitted into the rock.

prusik: a sliding loop of line attached to a rope that locks when weighted; any means to mechanically ascend a rope.

rack: the collection of gear a climber takes up the climb.

rappel: to descend a rope by means of mechanical brake devices.

runner: see sling.

scree: small, loose, broken rocks, often at the base of a cliff.

second: the second person on a rope team, usually the leader's belayer.

send: to cleanly complete a route.

slab: a relatively low-angle (significantly less than vertical) section of rock, usually with few large features.

sling: a webbing loop used for a variety of purposes to anchor to the rock; used to sling gear on; also called a runner.

sloper: a sloping hold with very little positive surface.

stance: a standing rest spot, often the site of a belay.

stem, stemming: the process of counterpressuring with the feet between two widely spaced holds; sometimes called bridging.

Stoppers: brand name for protection that acts like metal wedges placed in cracks and attached to the lead rope to limit the leader's fall if she loses her footing.

sustained: climbing adjective that indicates the continuous nature of the climb.

talus: an area of large rock fragments on a mountainside that may vary from house-size to as small as a small backpack.

toprope, toproping: a belay from an anchor point above that protects the climber from falling even a short distance.

traverse: to move sideways, without altitude gain.

verglas: extremely thin ice plastered to rock.

SOURCES

"Mind Games" from *Climbing* magazine, 1984.

"First to Climb Lizard Head" from *Outing* (November 1921) by Albert L. Ellingwood, 1921.

"New York Stories: Bouldering in the Big Apple and Beyond" from Rock and Ice, 1999

"The Schreckhorn" from *The Playground of Europe* by Leslie Stephen, 1871.

"Tawoche" from the *American Alpine Journal*, 1996.

"Exploring the Yosemite Point Couloir" from *Sierra Club Bulletin*, 1939.

"A Tale of Two Epics," unpublished, 2006.

"A Review of *Downward Bound*" from *Mountain Gazette*, 1975.

"The Ascent of Mont Ventoux" from *Canzoniere* by Francesco Petrarch, 1336.

"Freakers' Ball" from *Ascent*, 1974.

"An Ascent of Long's Peak" from *A Lady's Life in the Rocky Mountains* by Isabella Lucy Bird, 1879.

"The Great and Secret Show" from the *American Alpine Journal*, 1997.

"Mount Assiniboine" from *In the Heart of the Canadian Rockies* by James Outram, 1905.

"The Black Canyon with Kor" from *Mountain* magazine, 1976.

"Out with the Boys Again" from *Mountain* magazine, 1976.

ABOUT THE EDITORS

Kerry L. Burns grew up in Tasmania. As a geologist in the 1950s and 1960s, he explored the Tasmanian wilderness, the Australian outback, and the Cordillera Darwin in Tierra del Fuego in South America. His experiences in the coal industry of Australia and the United States led him to look for alternate sources of energy, and at Los Alamos National Laboratory he participated in the Hot Dry Rock geothermal projects at Fenton Hill, New Mexico, and Clear Lake, California. He is currently a geothermal energy consultant for projects in Australia, Europe, and North America.

Cameron M. Burns is a writer and editor based in Colorado. He has been writing about environmental, green architecture, energy, and sustainability issues since the late 1980s as a reporter/correspondent with various newspapers and as a contributing editor with numerous magazines. His essays, articles, op-eds, features, blogs, and other material on sustainability issues have been featured in publications and on websites around the globe. He is the editor of *The Essential Amory Lovins* (Earthscan, 2011); coauthor of *Building without Borders* (New Society Publishers, 2004), *Writing, Etc.* (Colorado Authors League, 2006), and *Contact: Mountain Climbing and Environmental Thinking* (University of Nevada Press, 2008), and author, coauthor, and contributor to more than two dozen books about the outdoors.